Advance Praise for
Climbing Out of the Wreck

"A survivor's tale indeed. This was like reading my story. The damage done to children by abuse and alcoholism is lifelong unless you are able to gather the *I'll show you*'s and take back your life. The child feels it's their fault, creating the continual cycle of destruction to prove again and again that you really are the piece of crap you've been programmed to believe. Very few find their way out, so deep is the damage. Christine Stein did it. If you've lived any version of this life, read this book and you will find hope, help, and inspiration to fix yourself and inherit the life you have always deserved. Her story has meaning. This is a great and important work."

—SUZANNE SOMERS, actress and author of *Keeping Secrets*

"It was a mixture of pain and pleasure reading Christine's journey. One of the most important things we do at the Barbara Sinatra Center for Abused Children is to give those who have been through these traumas hope. Christine's story is a gift that will do just that."

—HELENE GALEN, Chair of the Barbara Sinatra Center
for Abused Children

"I was completely blown away by this beautiful book. Once I started reading, I couldn't stop. It's an incredible saga and I was riveted from beginning to end."

—ADAM BELLOW, Editorial Director, All Points Press

"You will touch lives. Your book gives hope to millions of adults who were traumatized as children. Your very survival gives hope to those who wonder if healing is possible. Thank you for sharing your courageous story of victory."

—MARILYN VAN DERBUR, Miss America 1958, abuse survivor.
Author, *Miss America by Day*

"Wow. What an unbelievable saga, and so beautifully told. It's amazing Christine not only survived, but led a healthy and productive life having grown up amongst a gang of borderline personalities."

—JOEL SURNOW, creator and producer of the TV series *24*

CLIMBING
OUT OF
THE WRECK

CLIMBING OUT OF THE WRECK

A SURVIVOR'S TALE

CHRISTINE STEIN

BOMBARDIER
BOOKS

A BOMBARDIER BOOKS BOOK
An Imprint of Post Hill Press

Climbing Out of the Wreck:
A Survivor's Tale

ISBN: 978-1-64293-118-1
ISBN (eBook): 978-1-64293-119-8

Interior design and composition by Greg Johnson/Textbook Perfect

Post Hill Press
New York • Nashville
posthillpress.com

Published in the United States of America

To My Little Luck

Contents

Foreword

"A SURVIVOR'S TALE" INDEED—this was like reading my story. The damage done to children by abuse and alcoholism is lifelong unless you are able to gather the *I'll show you's*, and take back your life. Abused by a parent, the child feels they are at fault, creating a continuing cycle of destruction that proves again and again that they really are the piece of crap they've been programmed to believe. Very few find their way out—so deep is the damage. The real tragedy we are talking about in family abuse is the loss of potential. How many children of abuse are never able to achieve their true potential? How many doctors have we lost? How many lawyers have we lost? How many writers, teachers, professors? Most importantly, how many great parents are never formed due to the damage done from a childhood of abuse? And so, the sins of the fathers are passed on to the children.

In my own life I endured countless nights trembling in fear for my life and for that of my brothers, sister, and my mother, hiding in the dark closet, the sole purpose of which was to protect and help us disappear from the monster. We could hear the ranting and raving of the wild man downstairs—breaking things, throwing things like a crazy person. This was my father. We trembled in our silence, careful not to make a peep for fear of being discovered. Imagine! We were children! We had a lock installed on the inside of the closet door for these episodes that happened with almost every-other-nightly regularity. To survive, we had to have this closet refuge—a safe haven for when the terror struck.

Ask yourself, would an emotionally healthy person spend even one night living like this? Of course not, but in the cycle of abuse, you accept this as *normal*. So normal that as my mother would gather us together and say in those oh so familiar words, "Quick, get to the closet." We ran like sheep, up the stairs to our hiding place, and then stayed locked inside all night, perfectly silent so as not to be detected. We emerged in the morning like rats from a hole and never said a word…to anyone and, most importantly, never to our father. We did not want to give him fuel or ammunition for the coming night. None of us wanted to be "it."

The attacks were random, but you always knew your turn was coming—when you would be singled out as the object of his rage and venom. Our life at home was the dark secret we all kept, for fear anyone on the outside would know the awful truth. It was so shameful. How could anyone ever find self-esteem, or succeed in school or any endeavor, when you lived this life akin to being caged like animals? Even writing these words right now sends shivers down my spine. The real "sickness" was the ability we all had to put on a happy face. Protect the abuser. Protect the truth from being detected.

I am one of the lucky ones. It took the almost fatal accident of my little boy at five years old to finally get me to a therapist and change my narrative. God works in mysterious ways. The worst thing that ever happened to me turned out to be that which ultimately saved my life. I was so damaged, I never would have sought help for myself because I didn't feel I was worth it. I went to therapy only for my little boy—to help him stop the nightmares of being run over by that car again and again. I was distraught, helpless, and heard about the Community Mental Health Center.

I had given birth as a single teenage mother and had too much pride to ask for help. I never took anything from anyone, and was determined to make it somehow for me and my little guy. It was him and me against the world. The Community Mental Health Center provided its services and determined the charges based on ability to pay. I was charged one dollar a visit. The therapist, this angel in my life, said, "In order to work with him, I need to work with you." Little did I know she was the person who was going to save my life.

In the three intense years of working with her, she asked me repeatedly, "Where did you get the feeling that you were worth so little?" I could never answer her. I didn't know and didn't understand the syndrome. Then one day these words came out of my mouth...I said, "I don't know. I always thought I was useless, hopeless, worthless, nothing, and a big zero." I sat in shock hearing myself articulate this for the first time. Oh my god, I suddenly realized, this is what I had been told over and over and over as a child. I had been programmed. My father's constant bullying made me believe that I was as he said.

I look at the life I live today and it's nothing short of a miracle. As a girl, I didn't know I was smart and talented, and yet I've achieved the height of success as a Las Vegas entertainer, a *New York Times* bestselling author of twenty-seven books, an actress with sixteen years of primetime network television and number-one shows, a sought-after lecturer, and best of all, a person respected in my community.

Had I not gotten help, I never would have or could have achieved the life that I live today. I have been happily, blissfully, married to the same man for fifty years. I have three children and six grandchildren. I wake up every day filled with gratitude for the life I live, the love I have, the food I get to eat, the fact that I live in America, and that I have great health. Every day is a gift. Yet, without the necessary therapy by a woman who became the angel in my life, all that would've been lost. Socrates said it: "The unexamined life is not worth living."

To not do the work that gets you out of the maze is to allow the abuse to win. It renews the hurt over and over until it eats you from the inside out. But abuse can become a veiled gift. It can be your rocket fuel to win.

Christine Stein has done it with this book. She has had the courage to go back and look at what happened to her with all the pain and sadness, and to find a way out. It is essential for those of us afflicted with the pathologies of abuse to go back and truly feel our feelings—especially as an adult with perspective—so that processing the pain and seeing a clear way out becomes possible. If you've lived any version of this life, read this book and you will find hope, help, and inspiration to fix yourself and inherit the life you have always deserved. Christine's story has profound meaning, not only for herself, but for others as well. This is a great and important work.

—*Suzanne Somers*

CLIMBING
OUT OF
THE WRECK

This is my story as I lived it.
Only the names have been changed.

Prologue

O<small>N THE WAY TO MY MOTHER'S FUNERAL,</small> I vowed to myself I would not break down. I wanted to be strong in front of the family, and especially my son Michael, who had asked me to meet him at the entrance to the chapel so he wouldn't have to enter alone. Michael had been close to my mother, who had helped me to raise him after his father and I separated when he was still an infant. I was determined to provide the comfort for him that was often missing in the home I grew up in. Though anxious, at first, I felt confident I could hold myself together because the night before I had come apart and cried until I ran out of tears. But as soon as I brought my Ford pickup to a stop in the chapel parking lot, I was already short of breath and holding back the tears that were welling in my chest.

Michael had arrived before me and was waiting with his fiancée, Mary, a petite Filipina with jet black hair and eyes to match, who adored my son as he did her. After hugs, we pushed through the oversized chapel doors and into the room where dozens of mourners were gathering. As we crossed the threshold, I felt my chest tighten and my lips begin to tingle, familiar signs of a panic attack. To distract myself and hold back the pain, I began chewing on my lower lip. It occurred to me that some of my siblings must be in the room too, but I was unable to take in the crowd, because my eyes were fixed on the spot where my mother lay propped up in a salmon pink coffin.

Approaching the casket, I was struck by the way the mortuary people had managed to simulate a life that had vanished years before. Age and illness had ravaged my mother's once stunning looks, but here she was a picture of the beauty that hard living had taken from her, and finally at peace. They had even restored her delicate hands, which used to braid my hair and wipe away my tears, and make me feel loved. I reached for the one nearest and held it in mine as my thoughts travelled back in time. I was trying to think of the good things she had done for her children and block out the bad, which were bad enough that my oldest sister and youngest brother had refused to come to her funeral in protest.

During the ceremony, there were eulogies by a priest and two of my siblings. But aside from the good moments they remembered, nothing they said began to touch the realities of my mother's troubled life or our broken family. I was grateful for these omissions, and wouldn't have expected anything else. It was the way we all had made it to this point in our lives, since we all understood that to say anything approaching the reality would be dangerous.

All through the proceedings, and especially when they lowered her coffin into the earth, I thought how final it all is; how I will never have the chance to speak to her again; how our wounds will never be healed. This was on my mind and in my heart because four months earlier we had a terrible fight. It was triggered by her discovery that I had shared some secrets that were unflattering to her with my husband.

Our family was one in which silences about deeply troubling matters were normal, and indeed required. We behaved like members of a mafia, for whom secrets revealed could send us to jail or worse. The outside world teemed with threats, and the silences protected us. The family *omertà* was a code my mother had drilled into us from the time we were little, enforcing it with threats of her own, shaping our lives in ways I was still trying to understand.

"How *dare* you talk about our family and me to *anybody!*" my mother had screamed when she learned about the breach.

"When I am in pain," I said, desperately trying to defend myself, "I have a right to share my pain with my husband."

She would have none of it. "You have no right to share *our* privacy with *anyone*," she snarled back. "How could you *do* this?"

I did not want to fight with her and left many things unsaid out of fear this would only provoke her more. But the effect of this was to give her the upper hand and turn me into a supplicant seeking her forgiveness. Over the next weeks and months, I tried many times to reach out to her, telling her how sorry I was, and how I hoped we could put this past us, but to no avail. It was not the first time she had laid down the law to me about telling things she didn't want others to hear, or that she reacted to a transgression of mine with hurtful rage. The only difference was that, when I was young, her reaction was often physically violent, hitting me with a fist or clothes hanger, beating me in a rage until my father intervened. The little girl who was the target of these assaults could not fight back and would have done anything to make her happy and get her to relent. Now the adult could not forget those memories or the fears and loneliness that accompanied them.

Three months after our confrontation over my betrayal, her failing health reached a point where she had to be checked into the hospital. Although she didn't—and wouldn't—ask me to come, I drove the two hours to see her, wracking my brain along the way for words to appease her and make our conflict disappear. Even though I felt I was right in every fiber of my being, the little girl in me kept saying: *You must be wrong. You have to make her happy again. Do whatever it takes for her to forgive you.* I tried in earnest to heed this voice, to focus on the good things she had done and give her what she wanted. But I could not suppress the memories of the past, or her brutality when I could not defend myself. It bothered me that we both knew we were approaching the end of our time together, yet she was willing to wage this war and scorch the earth between us.

When I entered the hospital room and saw how weak she was, my heart went out to her. But as soon as she saw me, she turned away. Despite the hurt, I said nothing and

4

the room remained still for what seemed hours until my brother, Tommy, arrived. When he came, she immediately directed her attention to him, and shut me out again. While they were talking, I sat down, unnoticed at the end of the bed and began rubbing her feet. When there was a break in their conversation, I said, "Mom, you know I love you."

She started to cry. "I love you too," she replied, but almost immediately followed with an accusation. *"Why did you do what you did?"*

I knew that if I responded it would only incite her again, so I said nothing. In the silence that followed, I searched for words to make her feel she had me back under her control. But try as I might, I couldn't manage the complete surrender she needed. I was no longer a child and I could not bring myself to pretend otherwise. Since neither of us could bury the wound, I had to resign myself to the fact that this was the way it was going to finally be. There would not be time or life sufficient to retrieve it.

I stood up to leave and bent over to kiss her. "I love you mom," I said, "but I have to go."

She looked up at me. "I love you too, but…"—and here, steel entered her voice—"…I'm still *very* upset with you." I turned to say goodbye to my brother and left. A week later, she was gone.

It was her final rejection. She had left me to deal with the hurt and try to come to terms with the questions that had planted themselves in the center of my life: Who was this woman who gave love and withdrew it so coldly? How, finally, was I to feel about her, to love her?

Gigi

My mother's name was Gigi, but when she was little everyone called her "Cotton Top" because of her bonnet of platinum hair. My sandy blonde hair is one of the legacies she bequeathed me. As soon as Cotton Top was able, she was helping with chores on the family farm, especially with milking the cows, a task that she loved. When she was only two, my grandparents put her on Rosie, a chestnut quarter horse with three white socks. As she grew bigger, they became inseparable, and Cotton Top could be seen every day riding Rosie around the property. One day, she was playing in the barnyard when Rosie turned her head suddenly, hitting the little girl in the face. A horse's head is very hard and the blow knocked the child out. It was completely unintentional and Cotton Top recovered quickly. But when her father found out, he flew into an alcoholic rage, grabbed his shotgun, took Rosie out in the field and killed her.

My grandfather, Byron, was an angry man and also a stubborn one. When the deed was done, he refused to bury Rosie and left her body in the field to rot. The next morning, Cotton Top went to sit with her dead friend. She sat there all day, and cried. No one could get her to leave. When night came, they went out and dragged her in. But the next day, she was out in the field again, hugging Rosie and crying. This went on until my grandmother, Leoti, forced my grandfather to get his tractor and drag Rosie's body to the far end of the property and bury her.

Cotton Top was all of ten when this happened. I was deeply saddened by the story, which my mother only told me after I had become an adult and had acquired a horse of my own. Listening to her tell her story, and reflecting on it afterwards, I don't think she ever recovered.

Despite her good looks and talents, Cotton Top never had much of a chance in life. Her mother, Leoti, a Cherokee Indian, had married an abusive alcoholic from a wealthy family of German-Irish descent. Leoti bore him five daughters but finally left him because of his cruelty to her and her children. For reasons I could never understand, she left the children behind when she departed the household. This was another traumatic event in Cotton Top's young life. She was thirteen when her mother put her in the hands of the harsh man who had killed her Rosie.

With her mother gone, Cotton Top put away childish things and entered the world of adults. She began dressing seductively, taking advantage of the fact that she was a stunning girl with a fully developed figure and a demeanor the family called "sassy" and men found sexual. She put on high heels and dark red lipstick to provide a striking contrast to her platinum hair and sought out the bar night life. It was there she met a handsome man on the make, who was twice her age, named Marco Rossi. Marco was also an alcoholic and a physical abuser of women. He cheated on Gigi regularly and, when he found out that she had lied to him about her age, beat her mercilessly, splitting her lip and turning her black and blue. She left him many times over the ensuing years and had revenge affairs, but she always came back. Then, at fifteen, she discovered she was pregnant.

Gigi was a smart and curious youngster who loved school and had done well in her studies. But when she became pregnant, she was forced to quit. Still, she was so determined to educate herself that after her baby, Timmy, was born, she went back and graduated, despite the fact that she had little support at home. She had to buy her graduation dress from a thrift store and borrow the money from my grandfather, who was in jail for a drunken bar fight. After she graduated, she got a job, but was hit by another tragedy that she was never really able to overcome. Timmy was diagnosed with a heart defect that the doctors couldn't fix and died in his third year of life.

Gigi and Marco kept their liaison going long enough to have three more children who were still little when they agreed to separate for good. Shortly after the separation, Marco was felled by a heart attack and died at the age of thirty-two. Gigi was able to cope as a single parent with help from her mother, who had returned to the neighborhood after the divorce.

To support her little family, Gigi went to work in a food company where she caught the eye of the boss, an elegant charmer named Henry McCardle. The two became lovers and he soon bought a house for her and the children, which he kept in his own name. He also brought two children of his own into the household, increasing its youthful population to five. The boy, Joey, had a swimming accident when he was very young, which left him with brain damage. The older girl, Helen, left the family when she became eighteen, and never returned except to look in on Joey who had been put in a special facility for the "mentally challenged." Gigi and Henry went on to have three children of their own—Rick, Katie, and Janie. I never asked my mother why she had so many children, though it seemed a natural question since, like Marco, Henry never married her and was only intermittently at home.

When I was just a toddler, Gigi and Henry sent me to live in Temecula with my Aunt Nancy and my grandmother, Leoti. The two years I spent with them contain some of my happiest memories. My Aunt Nancy was married to Gene, a full-blooded Indian who was dark and handsome. I have vivid memories of Uncle Gene taking time to play with me and teach me to tie my shoelaces. He was a serious alcoholic but a kindly one, at least at home. Outside, he was less controlled, and long after I was gone from their household, he was killed in a bar fight at the young age of thirty-eight.

It was a two-hour drive to Temecula from where Gigi and Henry lived in Los Angeles, and their visits were infrequent. They never explained why they had sent me away, or why they came to get me two years later and took me home. When they came for me, I didn't want to leave. I clung to my grandmother and cried, but Gigi peeled me off her and put me in the car.

For many summers after that, I was sent back to Temecula with my sister, Katie. We would stay with Aunt Nancy and her three daughters, who were a few years older. One day when I was seven and Katie was ten, the girls decided that we would all go bowling. On the way, we stopped off at my grandfather Byron's house, where the family dog had a new litter of six puppies. I loved animals and began to play with them. Seeing this, my grandfather asked me if I would like to stay. Although I was a little afraid of him, I said yes, because I wanted to be with the puppies. My sister Katie went on with the older girls, and I stayed behind and played all day with the puppies by myself.

When it was time for dinner, my grandfather put a ham sandwich on the table and offered it to me. I took a bite of it and immediately put it down. My mouth was burning. For some reason my grandfather had put hot mustard on the ham. When he saw me put it down, he frowned and in a stern voice said, "Eat it," and then stared at me some more. I took another small bite, but it burned again. I looked up and saw that he was watching me. I couldn't understand why he was making me eat it and was on the verge of tears when he got up to go to the bathroom. While he was gone, I took the sandwich and threw it in the garbage.

After his divorce from Leoti, my grandfather had remarried. His new wife was nice but was more like a stranger to me. That night when I went to bed, my grandfather's new wife crawled in with me. I had never slept in a bed with an adult before and didn't understand. When I came down to breakfast in the morning, I saw the ham sandwich I had thrown away on the table, waiting for me. My grandfather had found it in the garbage, and put it back on the table, and made me finish it.

When Gigi found out that I had spent the night at my grandfather's house, she was furious and screamed at my sister and me. I didn't understand why she was so angry or why she kept asking, "What happened? What happened?" I didn't know what she meant. It was not until I was in my twenties that Gigi told me that my grandfather had molested his own daughters and got Nancy pregnant, and forced her to have an abortion. When I heard this, I understood why his new wife had stayed with me. But this knowledge made it even more difficult for me to understand how Leoti had left my mother and her four sisters behind when she fled his household. Gigi also told me that, when my grandfather's mother found out what he had done, she disowned him and when she died, although the family was very rich, she left him only a single dollar in her will. What my mother didn't tell me at the time was that my grandfather had molested her too.

I cherish the memories of my mother's concern for me over the incident at my grandfather's house. It is one of the reasons I have loved her through all the chaos and conflicts of our life together. But even the good moments we had often ended in bitter disappointments. When I turned six, she told me I could stay home from school because we were going to celebrate my birthday and make a cake together. Having time with her alone was special in itself and making the cake together even more so. It was a white cake with coconut frosting and cherries on top, which she let me pick out of a fruit cocktail cup she had bought. I had so much fun that day and felt so loved. When my brothers and sisters came home from school, and my mother made me the center of attention when the candles were lit, it brought me a happiness that has stayed with me to this day.

But when the cake was eaten, she got up and left the table abruptly and went to her room to dress. She had made plans to go a local bar that evening with a female friend. When she told me this, I was heartbroken. I didn't want her to leave. I didn't want my birthday to end. I wanted her to stay home and watch movies with us. From past nights when she went out on the town, I knew that a bar night meant she would not come home before the morning hours, and when she did, she would be wasted. She would come in loud and abusive, as though she did not have sleeping children in the house. She would flip on the radio, curse out loud, and make demands that woke us all up. We dreaded these late-night entrances because we were unable to go back to sleep and would be tired at school the next day.

I started to cry. I was just finishing my coconut cake as the salt tears dripped onto my lips. I begged her "Please, mom, don't go. Please stay with me." But it was futile. She was not going to give up her adult pleasures and had no intention of changing her mind.

"There'll be other times we'll have together," she said to pacify me, and left.

My mother drank too much generally, and one evening in that sixth year, she became so intoxicated that she fell over on me and broke my collarbone. Even in her drunken state, she was visibly upset by what she had done. But her contrition did not lead to any changes. She was a belligerent drinker, daring anyone to try to curtail her excesses, which tended to coincide with my father's absences. On one such occasion, when Henry had been gone for two weeks, she was drinking while getting dressed for "PTA night" where she was scheduled to meet with my sister Katie's sixth grade teacher to discuss her school progress. You wouldn't know that was the agenda, however, by the way she was dressed, which was as though she was going to a party. She had put on a tiny skirt and high heels, and a form-fitting pink sweater with big hoop earrings. She and her girlfriend were planning to celebrate at a local bar after the school night.

My sister, Katie, who was all of twelve, was an extremely pretty little girl with long blond hair, blue eyes, and beautiful olive skin. As she watched the women downing vodka shots while they finished their eyelashes, she grew increasingly concerned, and pleaded, "Mom, slow down. Slow down." But the women ignored her. When their makeup was complete, they left to go to the school night.

A half hour later, they were back. They had returned to pick up Gigi's purse, which she had left behind. The meeting with Katie's teacher had gone badly. As soon as Gigi stepped into the foyer, she went over to Katie and groused, "Your teacher is a real piece of fucking work." (Foul language was a second nature to her.) "She accused me of being drunk and neglecting you. I told her to fuck off." Katie and I were horrified. While we stood there, wondering what Katie's teacher would say to her tomorrow, Gigi grabbed her purse and started out the door. When she reached the threshold, she turned around to give Katie a last instruction: "When you go to school tomorrow, you set your teacher straight."

When the two women left, Katie was shaking and said to me, "I'm scared to go to school tomorrow."

By the time this incident took place, young as I was, I already knew that I had two mothers—a good, comforting one whom I loved, and a mean, foul-mouthed drunk who could withdraw that love without warning, whom I feared. All I could do was wait the bad one out and hope the good one returned soon.

Even as a child, however, I had a sense that my mother's abusive behavior came from a deep reservoir of pain. One night, my younger sister, Janie, and I were sitting in the living room with Henry when my mother came staggering in with the same girlfriend, who went over to Henry and in a whispered voice said, "We dropped acid and Gigi had a bad trip."

I didn't understand what this meant, but Henry was telling my mother, "Lie down, lie down. You need to go to your room and lie down."

I followed her as she went to her bedroom, but when I opened the door, she was hysterically stabbing the air with her finger shouting "Timmy's there! Do you see him? It's Timmy!"

I looked around for her lost child, but saw no one. "Where, mom? Where?"

Without looking at me, she stabbed the air again and said, "Timmy's right there." Now I was getting really scared. Suddenly, she turned towards the corner of the room, pointed again and screamed, "There's a man over there!"

I fled from the room and ran to my dad. "She's acting so weird, and I'm scared," I cried. "She says Timmy's in the room with her."

Looking annoyed rather than alarmed, Henry got up from the sofa and went toward the bedroom. I started to follow him, but he told me to go back and closed the door behind him. I heard him shout, "Lie down. Lie down," and then there was silence.

While there were eight children in our household, we were really two families, separated by age and fathers. There were Henry's five children, including the soon-to-be-departed Helen, and then there were Marco's offspring who were older than all of us, except Helen. The older Marco group were teenagers when the rest of us were still in elementary school and were out of the house by the time we were adolescents. Because of the age difference we looked on them as something of a different species—not children like us, but young adults. They were also a caution to me, since they quickly set examples of the negative impact our family behaviors could have on our lives.

When Marco's oldest son, Tommy, was in the ninth grade, Gigi got a call from the school office. The school principal and Tommy's teacher were on the line. They told Gigi they needed to have a meeting with her about Tommy's behavior. When the meeting took place, they told her he had anger issues and was disruptive in class. Then they asked whether anything in particular might be bothering him.

Tommy's class had been given a project to compose a poem and draw a picture to illustrate it. Tommy's poem went like this:

Birdy, birdy in the sky,
Birdy birdy up so high.
When you fall
I'll smash your fucking brains,
Birdy Birdy in the sky.

The picture he had drawn to illustrate this "poem" showed a bird on the ground with its brains smashed. Tommy used a red felt pen for the blood, which was splattered all over the bird's head and body. I found it quite disturbing when my mother showed it to me years later. While she didn't show the picture to us children at the time, she did tell us how she handled it, indicating how proud she was of her response. Tommy's principal had said to her, "Your son has rage in him. We have to figure out what to do."

To which she replied: "This is fucking ridiculous. Let's not go fucking overboard. We'll take care of this at home."

At home, Tommy adopted the family line. "I just did that to shock her," he explained. "It was nothing." And that is how it was left.

We all knew that the teacher and the principal were right. In the neighborhood, Tommy's rage was famous. He was always in street fights and had the scars—broken nose, busted elbows, bloody knuckles—to show for it. When he had just finished the tenth grade, his behavior escalated into something serious.

We had no central air in the house, so on hot summer nights, my younger sister, Janie, and I slept on the living room couch under the fan. One night, there was a pounding on the front door that woke us up. When my mother opened it, six policemen came charging in looking for Tommy. Gigi was screaming. They charged past her and into all the rooms. "Your son tried to derail a train. Where is he?" But Tommy was gone. He was hiding.

When he came back two nights later, my mother met him on the porch and said, "Tommy, you can't do this. You have to give yourself up. Henry will get you a lawyer." The police came and took Tommy to jail. He had two accomplices in the train derailment, which was the brainchild of an eighteen-year-old. At the trial, they were found guilty. Tommy was sentenced to Juvenile Hall, where he stayed for months, and then had a term of probation.

My mother reigned over our family chaos—and played a prominent role in engineering it. She was a beautiful woman with high cheekbones from her Cherokee lineage and an hourglass figure that she highlighted with skirts that were too short and necklines too low. Her hair had browned since she was little, but to keep her luster, she had her little girls bleach it to a Marilyn Monroe blonde. She flaunted her sexuality wherever she went and was the talk of the neighborhood, not least because she often wore only a long T-shirt with no underwear when she was out in the yard. When she stretched to hang clothes on the line her cheeks would often show to the consternation of the neighborhood women, whose husbands often came out to ogle her. The neighborhood children were constantly telling me "Your mom's so hot," and other comments that made me extremely uncomfortable. I hated how sexually she dressed, and was constantly embarrassed by her behavior. She was so pretty she didn't have to go around half-undressed to attract attention, and I was unable understand why she did.

From a very early age, I had so many mixed emotions about my mom. The fact that she made us notorious as a family was one. It reinforced our sense of being alone in a hostile world, and made the code of silence she imposed on us a necessary safeguard. But the same sexual behaviors were also a source of neighborhood envy, and thus a source of power to us. Our next-door neighbor was a very religious woman who held Sunday school sessions for the local children. When I was seven, I attended her Bible class. She was a tall, heavy-set woman with wide hips and plain features who dressed very conservatively. On this particular morning, she looked directly at me, causing me to lower my head, out of shyness. In a deep, drill sergeant's voice she said, "Christine, when I look at you, why do you look to the ground? You know that's where the devil is. You and your family are with the devil."

When I heard these words, I ran out of her house and over to ours, where Gigi was in the kitchen in a pair of shorts and a pink form-fitting sweater, familiar cigarette in hand. When I told her what the neighbor lady had said—that we were all with the devil—she exploded. "What the fuck!" she said, and grabbed my arm. We went flying out the front door and over to the neighbor's house. Gigi banged on her door. When it opened, the neighbor appeared. She was much bigger than Gigi was, but I saw the fear in her eyes. "Who in the hell do you think you are to tell my kid that we're with the devil?" my mother spat at her. "You can tell your fucking husband to stop whistling at me and staring at my daughters in the backyard." The Sunday school teacher was petrified, and speechless.

As we left, Gigi asked me, "Why do you go over there?"

I was at a loss for an answer. "I don't know," I said, "She gives me Kool-Aid and cookies."

This set Gigi off again: "I'll make you fucking Kool-Aid and cookies. Don't you ever go over there!" It was all so embarrassing to me. But I was proud of my mom. She had stood up for me and the family.

There were other bewildering episodes. Once I was old enough to understand such things, I hated that Gigi and Henry had indulged in sexual talk in front of us when we were younger, oblivious as to how it might affect their underage children. When Janie and I were five and six, Henry brought a nude calendar home. "Come over here kids," he said, and flipped the pages for us. "Look at all these ladies. Aren't they pretty?" Then he put his finger on one of the naked women, tapped the picture and said, "You see this lady? I like those nipples. Go and take this to your mother and tell her that these are my favorite nipples." It felt weird, but Janie and I took the calendar and ran to show our mother. Our thinking was: *this is what our dad wants us to do.* When we presented Gigi with the picture, she looked at it and said *huh* in a dismissive sort of way. It was as though it was all perfectly normal.

Henry was six-feet-tall with sandy hair, blue eyes, and broad shoulders. He came from a sophisticated, well-off family. His father was a businessman, and his brother was a commercial airlines pilot, while his mother taught French in high school, and kept a spotless house. Henry was a businessman too, and had become the head of the sales division of a national company. It was a job that took him away from the house regularly, often for long periods of time. As we grew up, we quickly learned that his absences were not all about business. One time, he said he was going on a company trip for five days. When he returned, we all piled into his car to go supermarket shopping. Janie and I were excited that he was home and taking us shopping, but when my mom opened the trunk of the car to put in the groceries she found a key from a local motel, and immediately confronted him. "You didn't go on a fucking trip," she screamed. "You've been in a local motel fucking a whore." I hated it when they fought, so I made up a story on the spot to stop it. I told them that I had found the key in the parking lot and thrown it into the trunk. As soon as I said this, the fight ended. Henry looked relieved and let my lie stand.

I was all of eight at the time, too young to make sense of this or of my mother's outbursts. Shortly after Helen became eighteen and left the household for good, Gigi and Henry had one of their numerous fights while Janie and I watched. "You whoremonger," she railed at him. "You fucked Helen."

Janie and I thought it meant kissing, but the harsh, impenetrable word stuck in my head.

Henry's infidelities, as I was to learn in the years ahead, were numerous and unending. To compound the indignities, he bought several of the women houses more expensive and more spacious than ours, while keeping the properties in his name. One of his flames was a Hawaiian dancer, Leilani, who became the occasion for regular trips to the islands where he claimed to have business accounts. At one point, he decided to take Gigi to Hawaii to the very resort where Leilani danced for tourists, although he didn't go so far as to actually introduce them. Meanwhile, Leilani had grown suspicious about who Henry was. He had told her he was divorced with two grown children, but he never took her to California when he went there on "business trips." She couldn't figure out why, so she did a search of his things and found our home telephone number.

When Leilani called, Henry was away and Gigi answered the phone. It didn't take long for the two women to begin comparing notes. When Gigi found out that Henry had bought a house for Leilani and that she had a son, she exploded. "That fucker. Let me tell you I am not an ex-wife—he didn't have the decency to marry me either—and I have a shit load of kids here to take care of."

Gigi bided her time and took her revenge. It began with an accident she had trying to ride a tricycle while she was drunk. Amused by her inebriated state, some of the neighborhood teens had dared her to ride one of the trikes that were spread around our yard. Naturally, she took up the dare, toppled over, and broke her forearm. That's when she met Dr. Morris, a semi-bald Jewish man who promptly fell in love with her. "I like you. I want to call you," he told her on her first visit. "You are one of the most beautiful women I've ever seen." Their affair went on for years. The trysts would take place in his Porsche, in his office, hotels, and even in our home when Henry was away.

She would say to us, "Everybody go outside and play. I don't feel well and Dr. Morris has come over to give me a couple of shots." Then they'd go into the bedroom and lock the door. We weren't fooled. But because we were so young, we thought it was about kissing.

Looking back at my mother's behavior, I often wonder if it wasn't in some way her search for a youth that was taken away from her too soon. The same could not be said for Henry, who had grown up in a loving well-to-do family and had nothing like the traumas in his life that she did. Whatever the causes of their behavior, I came to think of my parents as adults who never grew up.

What was so confusing to me was that, amidst the chaos and lack of connection, we did have great times as a group that made us feel like a regular family. The most memorable of these were trips we took to the mountains together, or to Disneyland and Knott's Berry Farm. Topping even those was the yearly ritual in which Henry would rent a house for us for four weeks in Redondo Beach. We would pile everyone into a three-room cottage on the beach, put sleeping bags on the floor, and have real family time. Henry would blow up rubber rafts for us to surf with, and then take all of us to the little beach town and buy us hamburgers and cokes. These month-long vacations are among my cherished memories. It was the good side of Henry that made us all love him.

Of course, even in these pleasures, the dark side was ever present. One summer, my mother's sister, Betty, came to stay with us. Betty had been a beautiful young woman with long dark hair and the family's signature high cheek bones. She was an excellent rider and a ribbon-winning "jumper." She became a catch for a very wealthy man who married her when she was only nineteen. They bought a large ranch in Utah with twenty thoroughbreds and warmbloods to train as hunter-jumpers, which Betty rode in horse shows.

Betty's story was also a famous family tragedy. On her wedding day, my grandfather Byron who had molested all his daughters when they were little children, came over to her house in the morning, drunk. He asked Betty why she was not going to have him give her away and then brutally raped her. The toll on Betty was great. After this trauma, she became an alcoholic, eventually succumbing in middle-age to cirrhosis of the liver.

On this particular vacation, when Betty came to stay with us at the Redondo beach house, things went well for a while. But then the three adults got to drinking and their gathering suddenly blew up with them all screaming at each other. Somehow it had come out in the drunken talk that Henry had had an affair with Betty. My mother went crazy on both of them, until they left. It ruined our summer.

A Turning Point

WITH SO MANY KIDS in our house we had lots of pets, including six or seven dogs who lived in our backyard. One of the dogs was mine—a black wire-haired mutt with a Schnauzer face and a white blaze on his chest. His name was Barney. I used to dress Barney in little clothes and put bonnets on his head and take him to bed with me. He was kind of ugly, but he was mine and I loved him. One afternoon, when I was eight, I came home from school and didn't hear the dogs barking from the backyard as they usually did when someone approached. Only two of the dogs were inside, so I went through the kitchen and opened the sliding door to the yard. There were no dogs in the yard. They were all gone. I went around the side of the house to see if the gate was open, but it wasn't. Then I heard a door slam and someone moving about inside the house and knew it was my mother.

When I caught up with her, I saw she had been drinking and was upset. I told her I couldn't find Barney or the other dogs and asked where they were. In slurred syllables she told me she had called the pound and the animal control officers had come and taken them all away. Then she tried to assure me it was for the best, but I was horrified. My mind was filled with images of Barney in the pound, and thinking how scared he must be, and how scared I was that they were going to put him down. I was in terrible pain. I cried and cried, and ran out into the backyard to Barney's doghouse because I didn't want to believe what had happened and didn't know what else to do. But, of course, he wasn't there. I went back inside, still crying, and through my tears and with all my might, begged my mother to please let me go to the pound to get Barney back. "Please mom, please. I'll do anything if you let me keep him." But she was unmoved and said no, that wasn't going to happen. A door had been shut that I could not open. My Barney was gone.

My mother had done it because she was angry. She was furious with Henry who had been away for a month. Abandoned and alone with all the dogs and children, she must have suddenly felt it was too much for her to cope with and decided to take out her frustration and rage on us.

Throughout my childhood, the memory of this incident was unbearable. Long afterwards, when I thought about what she had done, it occurred to me that her own father had set a terrible example from which she could not break free. Young as I was, I resolved then and there that my own path would be different. I would never do to my children what she had done to me.

I had no idea that other families did not have dark secrets or suffer inexplicable cruelties like mine. In my eyes, my family was normal, and when I didn't follow its rules, it was I who was wrong. Consequently, as a youngster, I was generally trying to heal wounds which I thought I had probably contributed to, and suffer quietly when bad things like this happened.

It was soon apparent that the killing of the family dogs had more serious implications than the pain inflicted on me. As the passing days revealed, it was an acceleration of the downward spiral that my mother's life had become, which was slowly engulfing our household. Before she plunged into a sea of alcohol, my mother had been a very neat person and kept her house in order. She always had on her high heels, even when she was hanging laundry, and usually wore a tied blouse with short shorts to show off her shapely legs. She would hang the freshly cleaned sheets on the clothesline in the backyard and I would go up to them as they billowed in the wind and inhale their scent. Now the house was more and more in disarray, the smell of cigarette ash was everywhere and the drinking was non-stop. Before we went to school, she would give us money to buy buttermilk and lemons at the local store to soothe her stomach and deal with her hangovers. I was troubled by her behavior, but it didn't occur to me that I was losing her. I just thought she was overwhelmed by what was happening and would soon come back to herself. But she didn't.

A cigarette routinely dangled from her lips, but now she developed a habit of leaving the lit cigarettes on furniture and counters throughout the house and forgetting them. It made me nervous to see them smoldering, so I followed her, picking them up and stubbing them out in ashtrays. It made for a curious sight: an eight-year-old following behind her mother to prevent her from accidentally setting the house on fire. She caught me a few times and when she did, she would yell at me, "What the fuck are you doing? That's a good cigarette." Then she would send me to the store to buy a new carton. Her favorite brand was Camels and, for some reason, despite my age, the local shopkeepers sold them to me when I said they were for my mother, whom, of course, they knew well. One time, she left one of her cigarettes on the bed and set it ablaze. My brothers Tommy and Rick poured pots of water on the flames, but it was not enough and they had to call the fire department to come put the fire out.

All of us were disturbed by her drinking and disarray. Rick, who was eleven, would go around the house locating the spots where she stashed her vodka bottles and throw them out or fill them with water. When she found out, she screamed at him: "You little fucker, I'll beat your ass." I felt bad for Rick. But there was really nothing that I—or anyone—could do.

Then a thunderbolt struck our household. My sister Melanie, who was just sixteen, ran away. There were mysteries shrouding the lives of all my siblings, but those connected to Melanie were deeper and harder to unravel. Before she ran away, she came into the bedroom where Janie and I were playing with our dolls and told us she was leaving. In a tender voice, she said, "You know that I love you so much and if you ever need me I will be there for you." And then, "Are you going to be okay?" I was bewildered by what she said and so sad. I didn't want her to go away and I didn't know why she was. It would be several decades and we would both be middle-aged by the time she was able to share with me the dark secret that lay behind her flight.

Meanwhile, Henry was off on a business trip again. His frequent absences always raised the tension level in the house, but this time, it was to the boiling point. When he was about to return, the conflicting emotions of happiness to see him, pent-up anger because of his desertion, and what she suspected he was up to would often rise to the surface and Gigi would explode. He had been away when Melanie left and came back hours later than his promised return. I was in the house playing with some of my friends when I heard screams from my sisters and brothers, "Stop, Mom! Stop!"

I ran outside to see what the commotion was and there was my mother, very drunk, wearing nothing but high heels and a T-shirt, chasing Henry around the family station wagon. She was waving a butcher knife at him and shouting, "You motherfucker! Whoremonger!"

Dodging her slashes, Henry brushed off the accusations with his usual sarcasm, and taunts, "You don't know what you're talking about, woman. You're crazy!" which only infuriated her more.

While he was darting out of reach of the blade, Henry tried to calm his terrified children by making light of what was happening, "Go back in," he said. "There's nothing new here. You kids know your mother."

This elicited another shriek, "Fuck you, you whore-chasing sonofabitch!"

Her pursuit continued until the exertion finally exhausted her and the drama came to an end, except for a last crack Henry saved for his children, "What a way to be welcomed home."

Distressing as all this was for me, I embraced Henry's view that my mother was just drunk and exaggerating things. I accepted his explanation because not to do so would have left me with no adult to rely on and would have been more than I could handle. What I would learn many years later, when I was long into adulthood and had a family of my own, was that my mother's anger was not just about the lying and sarcasm, or even the women Henry pursued on the side, but an even darker secret buried deep in the heart of the family itself.

After a few months, Melanie returned to our home. She again drew Janie and me aside and in a maternal voice said, "I love you." But she didn't say anything about why she had run away and I noticed that around the house, she was distant and even hostile towards both our parents. Even though she didn't run away again, she hardly spent any time in the house and was always somewhere else with her friends.

No one ever told me why she ran away, but I heard my mother say, "Oh she's out of control. She's on drugs and wants to party all night." I accepted her explanation, even though I had a feeling it wasn't true.

Melanie had grown into a beautiful young woman, slender and shapely with blonde hair and high cheekbones. She was so stunning people would compare her to the movie star Raquel Welch. All my sisters were beauties. Helen, who had left the house when I was still a toddler—which was something I didn't connect at the time to Melanie's disappearance—was the first in our family to become Homecoming Queen at our high school, followed by Melanie and Katie. Leslie would have been one too, but she left school when she became pregnant in her junior year.

All this female charm did not go unnoticed among the boys in the neighborhood. The young men who hung around our house often said to me, "You come from a hot family." The boys would line up their cars in front of the house and my older sisters would get in. Janie and I quickly figured out that if we tapped on the car windows while they were busy with our sisters, the boys would give us candy to make us go away.

The fun ended when the older children began to flee the sinking family ship. As soon as Melanie turned eighteen, she was gone again. Marco's other children, Leslie and Tommy, had already found ways out of the home by getting married—Tommy after impregnating a fifteen-year-old and Leslie by having a child with a biker. The house was now half empty. My father, as usual, was away a lot and my mother took to staying more and more in her room, drinking and listening to records by Frank Sinatra and other singers of melancholy tunes. Her favorite was Patsy Cline's "Crazy," which she played over and over.

Breakdown

ALL OF THE CHILDREN had a sense of impending disaster, but none of us could have imagined what was about to happen. It began on an afternoon when I was thirteen and came home from school to find the house unusually quiet. I called out to my mom but there was no answer. As I walked into the hallway that connected the living room to the back of the house, I saw her running from one bedroom to another. She was stark naked. I called out, "Mom, what's happening?"

At the sound of my voice, she stopped and wheeled around to face me. Her hair was mad and she was wearing sunglasses even though we were inside. In a conspiratorial whisper, she said to me, "There are aliens in this house and under the floor and they're getting into my skin, and taking over everything!" I started to cry. She didn't seem to notice and said, "I want you to hear this, and be quiet. Put your ear to the floor and listen, *listen*. Can't you hear them? They're talking right now."

I was really scared. I ran to the phone and called Henry's office. As soon as I heard his voice, I broke down and, through my tears, told him what was happening. He said he'd be right home. Before he arrived, Rick, Katie, and Janie came in and I told them the situation. Gigi had locked herself in her room but unlocked it when Henry came and called to her through the door. As soon as he disappeared into the bedroom, shutting the door behind him, we heard them screaming at each other.

"What the hell's going on? Are you drunk again? How could you do this in front of these kids?"

Then her voice, shrill and hostile, came through the walls. "Bastard," she said back at him. "Who are you fucking now?"

The door opened and Henry came out red-faced, "Get food for yourselves," he ordered us, "Go out and play and ignore this. I hate to tell you, but your mother's a drunk. Ignore her."

For reasons I couldn't understand, he left her in that state for a week. I was so scared for her I didn't even want to go to school. I would go into her room and lie on her bed, and stay there while she listened to her Patsy Cline albums. Even though I didn't know what was happening, I sensed that this was beyond any of the episodes I had witnessed before, and for the first time, felt like I was losing her. Dr. Morris stopped by once during the week to give her some drugs, but sedating her was not going to solve the problem. The house felt like a pressure cooker that was just waiting to blow.

And it did. Katie and I were in my bedroom when we heard Henry call out, "Katie, Christine, get in here and help me!" We ran to the master bedroom and there was my mother, completely naked, her body painted red with cream rouge.

Her face, her breasts, and her stomach were smeared with it, and she was screaming at my father a curse she probably heard from my grandmother Leoti, "White man speak with forked tongue!" While she assaulted him verbally she was also jabbing at his throat with a jagged piece of glass she had broken off from her hand-held mirror. Henry grabbed her from one side, Katie and I from the other, and we held her down on the bed. In the midst of this struggle, she noticed Katie and me holding her and said in a plaintive voice, "My babies." I felt so sorry for her.

Our presence seemed to calm her a bit. Henry grabbed the broken mirror from her hand and said to Katie and me, "Keep talking to her, I'm going to make a call." I saw he was scared and it scared me even more to see that. He said, "Help your mother get dressed; we're going to take her to the hospital."

When he left, I turned and told my mother I loved her. "You look so pretty," I said. At these words, she seemed to snap back for a moment and replied, "I love you too, my babies." We dressed her, and walked her out. Rick and Janie came in and then the four of us got into Henry's car. On the way to the hospital, we kept telling her that we loved her, hoping that would bring her back. She was crying all the way, wailing like a baby. When we arrived at the emergency room, Henry went inside and some orderlies came out and grabbed her and tried to pull her from the car. But she was kicking and screaming and wouldn't get out. They pinned her down and held her head. All the time, she kept wailing and acting like a caged animal. We were all pleading with her, "Please. Please, mom. Get out of the car."

Eventually, they pulled her out and took her into a room. We could hear her through the door, still screaming. Henry took out some money and gave it to us and said, "Go get some candy from the vending machines and wait." Then he followed her into the room.

An hour passed, during which her screaming through the walls never stopped. I couldn't eat the candy we bought and just held it, wondering why her screaming wasn't stopping. I wanted somebody to make her feel better. We were all scared and asking each other: Why aren't they giving her medicine to make her feel better? Then the door opened and Henry came out and told us that they were going to take her to another place. They wheeled her out on a gurney. She was in a straitjacket and her face was so red it looked like it was on fire. She was screaming for her first child Timmy, whom she had lost. At that moment, I felt in my heart that from this point on, my life with my mother would never be the same.

They had strapped her down. Her hair was matted, and she was sweaty, and so worn out that she was reduced to whimpering, "Timmy, Timmy," and then, "I want to die. I just want to die." They put her into an ambulance to take her to a psychiatric hospital in Pasadena and we followed behind in the family wagon. She was crying as they wheeled her into the facility. Henry followed her gurney in and a lady came out to meet us.

When she saw the four of us children, she looked very sad and tried to reassure us, "Your mother's doing all right, and we're going to help her. She's going to stay with us for a while."

The lady led us into a game room that had a green velvet pool table. Two men in their twenties who appeared to be patients were already there. One of them had a moustache and a jet-black pompadour and looked like the television character "Fonzie." He was sitting in a corner, listlessly strumming a guitar. I didn't know it then, but his name was Clark Hassan and he was about to play a large role in my mother's life and mine.

Rick and Janie had started to play at the pool table when the other young patient began circling them in an animated fashion. He grabbed a pool cue and was jabbing frenetically at the balls on the table and then at Rick, who pushed him away with his own stick. This jousting looked like it was about to become serious when Rick said to Janie and me, "Get out of the room!" and we all left. We wanted to say goodbye to mom, but the lady intercepted us and said that was not going to be possible.

Driving home, it was very quiet. When we got there, we asked Henry when she was coming back. He said "Don't worry about it. They will make your mom better. Go watch TV." We were all exhausted and drained from the day's events. Henry retired to his bedroom. Not long afterwards, I followed him to the back of the house. I wanted to hug him, and I wanted him to hug me. But I could see through his door, which was slightly ajar that he was bent over and crying. At six-foot-two and weighing 220 pounds, Henry was an imposing figure. Normally, he was confident and sarcastic. It was the only time I had ever seen him so hurt and lost.

A week later, we went back to the hospital for a visit. I was so happy and excited. All I could think about was that I was going to see my mom and she would be coming home. When we got there, she was in a white gown and heavily drugged. Her eyes were disconnected and ghost-like. It was as though someone had taken her soul. Many years later, she and I talked about this first meeting and she told me that she was on a suicide watch and they had stripped her and tied her down for the whole week and kept her drugged. The first time they let her up was when we came to see her.

There are two types of families. The first are traumatized by crises like the one we were going through. They cry and suffer together and talk each other through it. The second, which is my family, is also traumatized, but dances around the truth. They pretend that nothing serious has happened and tell themselves, "It won't really hurt us." We had been taught not to talk about what happened to us or, if we did, to keep everything on the surface. We laughed about the crazy guy who attacked us in the game room; we laughed about the guitar player who looked like Fonzie. We talked about how mom had "flipped out" and when she might be coming home. We knew that the breakdown was serious, but we never doubted that she would be coming home.

I wanted to know why her breakdown had happened, and what problems the two of them had that might have led to it. But Henry never talked about such matters. It was always, "Your mom is going to be fine and will be coming home," neither of which was true.

Every day, I would get up to go to school but really didn't want to. I wanted to see my mom. The first visit to the hospital was repeated many times. I was too young to appreciate that it was, in fact, the drugs that were affecting her and coming between us. The lithium they put her on gave her a zombie look, veiling her beautiful blue eyes with a film I couldn't penetrate. It was as though someone had stolen her from me. When I asked Henry about her state, he would reassure me, "Oh, she's tired. She's been through a lot. She'll get better."

I didn't want to wait for her to get better. I wanted her to be better now. During our visits, I would hug her and cry, "Mom, please. I want you to come home. I'm scared. It hurts to be without you. It hurts to go to school. It hurts to eat. I want you to cook for me again."

When she heard this, she would just look at me and in a dreamy distant voice reply, "I love you too." But I could never get past the fact that it wasn't my mom talking to me. She was gone and I didn't know how to get her back.

Without understanding why, I suddenly found myself very alone. My fourteenth birthday came and went and she wasn't around to celebrate it. Even though the older siblings had left, our house still bustled with young people. But it was not the same; we were all pretending that nothing had happened. Our mother had just taken a long trip and would be returning soon. In my heart, I knew that was not true, that something terrible had taken place and everything had changed. There were so many questions I wanted to ask, but there was no adult to answer them. I couldn't even talk about it to my siblings. Like me, they were each trying to deal with it alone. The language we spoke in our family was incapable of addressing what had happened, not just to our mother, but to us all.

Weeks went by and brought changes to my mother's condition. But the changes were a far cry from Henry's assurances that she was going to get better and I began to feel like she would never come back. Henry was away a lot now, leaving us to ourselves—a houseful of kids. He had stopped taking us to see her, which made missing her even harder.

When I fell ill with a strep throat while he was gone, all my feelings of loneliness and need for her rose to the surface. My ear was on fire, my body was aching, and my throat so sore I could hardly swallow. I felt so weak and wanted to see her so badly, to get her comfort and help that I asked my brother Rick, who was nineteen and the oldest member of the household now, if he would take me to the hospital on his motorcycle.

When we arrived, they had moved her out of the bare quarters where they first put her and into a regular room. I took this as a sign that she was coming back to her normal state and my spirits rose. Henry had previously brought her clothes and personal things, and she and her young room-mate had put posters of rock stars on the wall and plants on the night tables in their new quarters. But I hardly saw any of this when I entered due to the disturbing image of my mother herself. She was made-up and dressed like one of my teenage friends. She was wearing a pair of hip-huggers and a button-up white shirt whose tails were tied, revealing her bare midriff. A cigarette was dangling seductively from her lips and she was chatting with her roommate and a young man in his twenties whom I recognized as the guitar player we had encountered when we first arrived. "This is my friend Clark," she said.

My throat was burning as I went towards her and pulled on her sleeve to get her attention. "Mom, I'm sick," I whimpered, but she didn't seem to hear. I tugged at her sleeve again, "Mom, I'm sick." I desperately wanted her to hug me and tell me what to do to make me feel better. My throat hurt so badly and my ear was still aching.

But she was more interested in the conversation with her roommate and Clark than how I felt and even annoyed that I had shown up. It was as though she didn't want her friends to know she was someone's mother. Or perhaps she didn't want to know herself. The words that then came out of her mouth changed our relationship forever. "What the fuck do you want me to do about it?" she barked. "Take some fuckin' aspirin."

I never felt so crushed. Tears came into my eyes and I turned to Rick and said, "I just want to go." We left together, and he drove me on his motorcycle to Dr. Morris's office. I cried all the way soaking my brother's t-shirt. When Dr. Morris finished examining me, he told me I had a strep throat and gave me a shot. After he administered the antibiotic and handed me a prescription, he asked me when my mother was coming home. I said, "I don't know. It feels like she doesn't want to come home." Then Rick and I left.

Back at our empty house, the full impact of what had happened set in. The realization came very suddenly and very finally. I couldn't stop thinking about what she had said and the contempt with which she had dismissed me when I was feeling so weak and needy. I was only in my early teens, but that night, I lost my childhood for good. I was no longer a little girl looking for love and direction because I knew there wasn't going to be any from the only person to whom I had ever been able to turn. There wasn't going to be a mom anymore to give me soup and crackers or watch over and comfort me. There wasn't going to be a mom whose arms I could run to. The woman who kept the house in order and was there to kiss and comfort me and tell me, "You are going to be fine, sweetheart," was gone. The alcoholic was gone too. The booze had been replaced by drugs. I realized I would have to build a relationship with a new person and find out who she was. But the bottom line for me was this: I am motherless; from now on, I will have to look out for myself.

Over the next weeks, I visited her several times with one or another of my siblings, but the scene never changed. She was always with her new clique and I couldn't get in. Each time I went, she was absorbed with her new friends and especially her new boyfriend, Clark. She was very sexual around him, conveyed in her gestures, her walk, and her wispy tone, which had the added effect of shutting me out. Each time I went to see her confirmed the feeling that this wasn't my mother anymore. This was a woman who didn't care about me and I wasn't going to fool myself into thinking she did so she could reject me again. Each visit was a reminder that I was on my own.

Moving On

WITHIN ME, A NEW RESOLVE was building. I was going to take charge of my life. Without really thinking about it, I began re-doing the house. I asked Henry if I could paint the living room and he agreed, probably thinking this would keep me occupied, or perhaps realizing that since there was not going to be a parent in charge, a fifteen-year-old might fill some of the vacancy. I recruited one of my school friends to help me. We brightened up the room by making it a lighter color and then moved on to the kitchen and the bedrooms, putting flowered wallpaper along the hallway as we went until we had redone most of the house. I took down my mother's living room shelf and removed her knick-knacks—the plates and pottery and Tequila bottle she had placed there. I took them all down, every reminder that this home had once been hers. And each time I did, and with each room I painted, I felt a little better.

When she finally left the hospital, Gigi didn't come home. Instead, she moved in with her new boyfriend Clark, who was living with his parents in Huntington Estates, the wealthiest neighborhood in Pasadena. The first time I visited her, I came with Janie and Rick. We were met at the door by Clark's mother, Rose, and as we stepped inside, were immediately awed at the grandeur of the place. The Hassans were Persian and the style they aspired to was opulent and grand. The ceilings were twenty feet high and from the door you could see to the end of an enormous room whose windows opened onto an estate of sloping lawns and gardens adorned with classical statues. It was the largest and most palatial home I had ever been in. The entry and living room alone were almost as big as our entire house.

While we were taking in its features, my mom appeared, all five-foot-three of her in a black form-fitting workout leotard and high heels. She was smiling and looked so pretty. But I knew in my heart that, while she seemed glad to see us, her real happiness came from having a twenty-five-year-old boyfriend, living in a millionaire's mansion, and having no children to take care of. I wanted to shout at her, "Just because you have this new life and can be fancy-free without children, doesn't mean we don't want to be your children." But it wouldn't have made any difference, and I said nothing.

Our house was more parentless than ever. Henry hardly ever slept there and was away a lot on "business." He would check in once or twice a week to drop off some groceries and see how we were doing. On one occasion, he asked me to come with him and buy the groceries, and then it became

"Here's some money to buy groceries and other things for the house." During the week, I would manage the household allowance—about twenty dollars—and we would try to visit the Pasadena residence on the weekend. When we did, Clark was always sedated-looking and half-asleep. On one occasion, Gigi complained that Clark's mother was using her as a "babysitter" to see that he "didn't do too much heroin or OD." We didn't fully understand what a heroin addiction meant. However, the three of us were quite amused at Clark's narcotic state and burst out laughing when, one time after shooting up, he teetered and tottered and then keeled over in the kitchen.

One day, my mom appeared unannounced at our house. When she came in, we chatted a bit and she seemed happy. But then she started taking in the remodeling I had done and the changes I made. "Who did this?" she asked in an ominous tone.

"I did," I replied just as I saw her eyes come to a stop on the wall where her shelf had been.

"You fucking little bitch," she yelled. "Who do you think you are, moving my shit?" I think she expected me to cower in fear as I always had when she unleashed her wrath.

But I was no longer the little girl she was used to pushing around. This time, I was angry too. "*You* don't live here anymore," I said defiantly. "Do you think time stands still?" She was shaking and I didn't know if she was going to hit me. But my answer seemed to give her pause and she didn't.

A week later, she came back to the house and then her visits became routine. She would come over in the afternoons after my ninth-grade classes let out. I was excited at the thought that I would see her, which showed that I hadn't quite put behind me the hopes that her transformation had dashed. As soon as school was over, I would race across the fields and down the sidewalks of the neighborhood to be there when she arrived.

She had found out from Henry that he gave me an allowance to buy groceries for the house, and suggested we do the shopping together. She said, "I'll pick you up and drive you," and I happily agreed. In the back of my mind were sweet memories of the family outings in the days long past. At those times, she would make picnic baskets for us and pack them with her lunch meats and fruit salad, and before it all, we would go shopping together for the ingredients.

When we got to the supermarket she said, "Give me the money," which I did. As we shopped, I noticed that she was buying day-old bread and the cheapest shampoo. When I complained, "We don't like that," she said, "Get over it, and learn to like it." Then I noticed that she had put a carton of camels into the shopping cart, which were obviously not meant for our weekly food ration.

I didn't say anything that day or for several visits afterwards. But when she started putting beer and vodka into the cart, which ate up half our allowance, I couldn't overlook it anymore. "Mom," I said, "you're taking food money meant for your children to buy vodka for your millionaire boyfriend." The minute the words left my lips I saw her nostrils flair and eyes narrow.

She didn't say anything while we were in the supermarket or when we loaded the groceries into the car. But once she had settled into the driver's seat and pulled out of the parking lot, she reached over and cold-cocked me in the face, splitting my lip. As she did so, she screamed at me, "*You're* not running this ship."

Hurt as I was, without thinking or measuring the consequences, I yelled back: "*You're* not running it. The only running you're good at is running out the door."

It took about ten minutes of gritted teeth amid a suffocating silence for us to get back to the house. As we drew up to the driveway, I was relieved to see Henry's car parked there. Knowing what was coming, I bolted towards the front door, blood dripping from my lip, and cried out to him. "She bought Clark vodka and beer and spent our grocery money!" I was running toward him and felt her close behind me. When those words came out, she passed me and ran inside where she grabbed a wooden mop handle from the kitchen. When I entered, she started beating me with the mop handle. The first blows caused me to fall backwards onto a kitchen chair. I tried to fend her off with my legs, which took the brunt of her attack and were stinging with pain.

I don't know what would have happened if Henry hadn't been there. He was furious and yelled at her, "Stop it! Stop it right now."

His intervention allowed me to flee to my room, where I heard them still arguing and Henry warning her, "You better stop it because this is child abuse." The warning seemed to have an effect because their voices suddenly became muted.

After a few minutes, she came back to my room with a look that was now contrite. She was crying, and saying, "I love you. I'm sorry." Then she wiped the dried blood from my face and surveyed the welts on my leg.

I should have been angry, but my first instinct was to reassure her. "I'm okay mom; it's all right." I was still trembling and in a state of shock. She stayed with me for a little while, comforting me and looking as remorseful as she was able, but I was still whimpering when she left.

After this incident, we all backed off. Henry increased our food allowance and my mother reduced the amount of money she took for cigarettes and alcohol. The beating had taken a toll on me and made me decide it wasn't worth fighting her over the portion she continued to take. Meanwhile, her visits increased to several times a week. I wasn't sure why, but I knew she had time on her hands since Clark's parents had made him take a job carrying messages in the real estate offices they owned. Even though she was coming over more frequently, she would always leave promptly at 2:30 p.m. to get back to Pasadena. I felt a deep sadness every time she left, another indication that I hadn't quite adjusted to the new world I had entered.

That spring, I got a job bagging groceries at a supermarket where I could work on weekends and sometimes after school. I was excited about this since it took me out of the house. I was so eager to take the job that I didn't think too much about the fact that the supermarket was about five miles from my house and I had no vehicle to take me there. Because Rick was working too, he couldn't drive me on his motorcycle except once in a while. So, I resolved to walk the distance. I would get off at about six or seven, when it was still light enough that I wouldn't be scared walking alone and be there within an hour. One Saturday, however, the manager called me and asked if I could take a shift until nine o'clock at night. I didn't want to upset my boss, so I said I could. Then I called Henry and told him the situation and asked if he could pick me up. He said, "No, I'm going to be out with Marge." Marge was one of his girlfriends.

What I wanted to hear him say was, "Yes, of course I'll pick you up. I don't want my daughter walking five miles through the streets alone at night." But I had grown used to the fact that I couldn't count on him to care about me that way. Or thought I had.

"Oh, that's no problem," I said about his date with Marge. But I really wanted to scream, "I'm only fifteen. I need a parent. I need my father to help me." I didn't do it because I didn't want him to be mad at me, so I said nothing.

My shift lasted until ten o'clock because they asked me to help clean up when the store closed. By the end of the shift, my feet were tired and swollen, but I thought I could still run fast if someone tried to harm me along the way. I just hoped that the road back would be well-lit and that it would be all right. As I walked the darkened streets, headlights of the cars kept flashing in my eyes. Every now and then, I had to stop because my feet ached so badly. Then I would run to make up the lost time. About halfway, I began to get really scared. Some men had whistled at me from the passing vehicles, and called out, "Hi, baby. Want me to take you home?" I was so scared I broke into a full run. I was thinking that one of them could stop his car and drag me into it and I would be gone.

Luck was with me, however, and I was able to run all the way to my street without anything bad happening. When I reached the house, I took a deep breath and said to myself, "I'm safe. It's ok." Then I noticed Henry's car in the driveway. My heart dropped. He wasn't at Marge's as he said he would be. He was sitting in the living room with my brother Rick. He had come over because Rick asked him to help him fix his motorcycle. Even though I should have known I couldn't expect anything different from him, this revelation stung me to the quick. It showed me how he actually cared even less than I imagined. I was still shaking inside from the fear of the walk and now I was confronted with the fact that fixing Rick's motorcycle was more important to him than I was.

When I looked at him he turned away, which showed that he knew very well what he had done. Neither of us spoke. We didn't have to. We never referred to the incident again. Why would we? Talking about what was really going on between us was not something anyone in our family did. We sucked it up and remained silent until a day came when the pain would erupt like a volcano.

One weekend, my mother dropped by the house with her boyfriend, Clark. Janie and I were sitting with them in the living room when she said, "Have you girls got into smoking weed when I'm not around?" and offered us some pot.

The two of us were taken aback by the question but I was able to summon an answer. "Katie does with her boyfriend, but we haven't."

We had seen our older siblings doing it and other kids in the neighborhood, so when she said, "Would you like to learn?" we said yes. Clark offered us a joint he had just rolled, and my mom said, "It's better that you do it first with me than with God only knows who else." I inhaled Clark's joint. It burned my throat and lungs, but then the drug took over and I grew calm. Even though I had asked for the joint, when I looked at Clark and my mom smoking it, I thought, "Wow. My mom is getting her kids high. What kind of mom does that?"

From that day, I began smoking weed regularly. The new habit brought relief from the pain I was feeling and made me want to do it more. But smoking also interfered with my plans to get myself in shape and be healthy again. In grade school, I had won two awards for physical fitness. One was signed by President Nixon as part of a National Health Council program to encourage exercise. To win the award, I completed a two-week program of runs, push-ups, and sit-ups. Those of us with the highest scores were given the awards at a special assembly. I was so proud when my name was called out and when I received the award signed by the president. I took the certificate home to my mom, who promised to frame it but never did and eventually lost it.

I liked exercise. It helped me stop thinking about the things that scared me. After the award contests were over, I had kept up the running and pushups and got so good that when Henry went with me to the track, as he sometimes did, I would lap him in our runs. But then all the drama and pain of my mother's breakdown happened and I stopped. When my mother left the hospital and started coming over for visits and I began my runs to the house to see her, I thought I would be able to resume the exercise routine. But now, I found relief in the weed and spent more and more time getting high. Janie and I would even get high together before going to school where we were amused that none of our teachers ever figured it out.

I was now approaching my seventeenth year and going to parties. Because I was pretty, I was popular and often found myself socializing with the wealthier kids, who seemed to have more access to weed. I still hadn't dated or been intimate with anyone. The traumas of our household had made me apprehensive about the chaos that could result from things you didn't foresee. To prevent this, I had formulated a strategy to avoid the potential pitfalls that lay ahead. One part of the plan was to be cautious about sexual encounters. Another was that I was not going to be a drug user like the "loadies"—as we called them—who brought the weed to the parties. I wouldn't think of dating any of the boys I met there, even though more than one made a pass at me. I would never think of taking a loadie seriously. My long-term strategy was to avoid ending up in a home like mine.

One day, my sister Janie told me about a boy she had met in school whom she really liked. He was an Italian kid named Ronnie who was six-feet-tall, a body builder and one of the school's star athletes, captain of the football team. I suggested to Janie that we go together to watch the football practice so she could meet him. Janie had long brown hair and shapely legs and, like all of us girls, a fine figure. Before we went, I helped her pick out an outfit that would look especially cute.

I really wanted this to happen for her. I decided to wear baggy jeans and no makeup to be sure that I was in the background.

When we got there, I told her to sit up front while I climbed four or five rows to the middle of the stands to look for a friend whom I knew would have some weed. When the football practice was over, Ronnie started coming over and I got a little giddy thinking my sister was going to get the guy she liked. But he walked right past her and came over to me. He perched his right leg on the bench beside me and started scratching the top of his head and said, "Hi. I always wanted to talk to you."

I thought he looked like a monkey scratching his head like that and was angry that he was hurting my sister. In the most dismissive tone I was able to muster, I said, "What do you want to talk to me for?"

He ignored the tone, and replied, "Oh I've always noticed you and always wondered what it would be like to have a conversation with you."

I looked over at my sister's face and knew that her heart was breaking, and said, "*Why?*"

But he persisted, "Well, I'd like to talk to you about just anything." Then, he said with a nervous laugh, "I'd really like to take you out sometime."

That made me even angrier. "I don't think so," I replied in my coldest voice.

The next day, he called the house. Rick picked up the extension and called out, "Christine, some guy's on the phone for you."

I picked up the other end and heard Ronnie's voice which was cracking, say, "Hi, it's Ronnie. I was just wondering if maybe we could all go out together."

In an emotionless voice, I responded again, "I don't think so."

As the words left my mouth, I heard Rick on the extension laughing. "What a chump! Loser!" he cracked into the phone and hung up.

When Janie came home, we all chuckled at what Rick had done. But the next day, Janie had a class with Ronnie and when we were alone together, she pleaded with me to reconsider. "I feel so bad for Ronnie. He couldn't look at me in class. He's super depressed."

She wanted me to care about him, but I didn't. "I don't know him," I said, "and I don't care to know him."

A week later, she came to me with an urgent plea. "Christine, you've got to talk to him. He came in with a cast on his hand and his friend told me he's so upset over you he rammed his fist into a wall. It's so bad, Christine. Can't I tell him he can hang out in a group with us? He's a nice person." I felt bad for Janie and couldn't turn her down, so I told her that would be okay, but I still wasn't interested in him.

Janie arranged the date. The plan was for us to meet Ronnie at the movies. When we got there, I sat myself as far away from him as I could. But a week later, I fell ill and Janie must have told Ronnie because he called me at home. "You know," he said, "I'm into physical fitness. I know all the best vitamins to make you healthy again. Can I come over and bring you some things to make you feel better?" I said okay to that, but when he came to the door I asked my mother, who was there on one of her visits, to open it for him because I didn't want to see anybody. He gave her four bottles of different vitamins and some healthy brownies, because he remembered I had said I liked brownies and then he left.

When he was gone, my mother came over to me. "He's so nice," she said, "He seems like a really sweet person. Why didn't you come to the door and talk to him?" This set me to thinking about the care he had shown for me. I decided to call him and thank him.

When he answered the phone, I told him I really liked the brownies and was getting ready to take the vitamins. After we talked a little more, he asked me if I would go out with him. I was feeling better about him, so I said we could do that when I was well. Over the next week, he called me several times and we talked about school and sports, and he told me about his family. I was particularly impressed when he told me that his family went to church every Sunday and his parents had been married for twenty-five years. I liked how normal they sounded.

When I recovered from my illness, I told him I was ready to go out. He came over to pick me up in a green Cadillac, which I promptly christened the "Green Hornet." He was wearing his school jacket with all his team letters, and we went up to Stimson Park where he gave me pointers at basketball, and then we had some lunch. We talked a lot, and I was feeling very good about how easily it went. When he asked if he could take me out to dinner, I said yes.

The dinner date was at Red Lobster where I couldn't find anything but a salad to eat since I didn't like fish. At dinner, he was alternately talkative and shy, a quality that appealed to me. Afterwards, he drove me home and parked the Green Hornet in front of my house. Then, in his shy mode, he asked if he could kiss me. He assured me he had brushed his teeth, and we both laughed since we had just eaten dinner. Then he leaned over and his lips touched mine. His mouth smelled like fish, but I overlooked it because I liked him.

Ronnie's personality was thoughtful and sweet which was especially attractive to me. The fact that he was a star athlete and a "big man on campus," on the other hand, was not something that was important to me as it might have been to others. What impressed me was his determination to be healthy and the fact that he didn't smoke weed, which became an inspiration for me to stop. His interest in physical fitness soon led to my exercising again and that made me feel even better.

Special treats were the Sunday dinners that were a ritual with his family, and to which I was regularly invited over the next two years. They were large affairs that included his two brothers, aunts, uncles, grandparents, and six cousins who gathered every Sunday for spaghetti, lasagna, and home-made pizza that his grandfather made. I loved listening to his family laugh. I loved the way they enjoyed each other and made plans to spend time together. It was the opposite of my home, and it was the family I wished was mine.

Our relationship was pretty innocent for the moral standards of the time, considering what was going on around us. We were together almost daily for five months before we made out—hanging out after school, going over to his house, going to the movies, taking hikes and attending his football games. It wasn't that he was sexually prudish or didn't want to go further. He told me how he loved my looks, my blonde hair, and high cheekbones and, of course, my full breasts. But when he made advances or tried to touch my breast, I would push him away and say, "I'm not ready." I was scared of losing control. My family was so sexualized and the consequences were forbidding. My sister, Leslie, had gotten pregnant when she was no older than I was then and my brother Tommy had become a father in his teens. My parents and siblings were often out of control and I saw the messes that caused and didn't want them for myself.

Eventually, Ronnie and I did get hot and heavy. Since we had no place of our own, we enjoyed our intimacies in the "Green Hornet." Sometimes, when his parents were gone, we had the luxury of making out in his home, but these treats were rare. One time when Ronnie came over to my house, he said he had saved up some money, so we could take a room in a nice hotel. The "hotel" turned out to be a Motel 6. We went there in the evening, and when we arrived, I noticed there were a lot of big rigs parked in the lot and truckers coming and going. What I saw made me a little nervous and I asked Ronnie if we were going to be okay. He told me his brother had said it was a good place to go. I wasn't fully reassured, and I was also shy, so I asked him to go into the office by himself and get the key. While he was gone, the traffic in the parking lot made me even more nervous.

When Ronnie emerged from the office with the key, he had a silly smile on his face, but my eye was drawn to the bald trucker who was walking behind him. He came up to Ronnie and said, gesturing towards me, "Do you have her for the night? Could you send her my way afterwards?"

When he heard this, Ronnie punched him in the face and pushed him to the ground. I was screaming and Ronnie was beside himself. As he got into the car, he said, "I can't believe my fucking brother would tell me to go to a place like this." I was touched by the way Ronnie had defended my honor. When I got over my fear—I was literally shaking with fright—the two of us were able to laugh about it. Being close to someone like Ronnie was very comforting.

Back home, things were different. One afternoon, my mother came over on one of her usual visits and wasn't feeling well. I told her to lie down while I finished the dishes I was washing, and then I would make her some chicken noodle soup. A little later, Henry stopped in. He asked how she was feeling and I told him. Then he said, "I hear you have a new boyfriend."

I said yes, and my heart picked up that he might be showing an interest in me. But the tone of his voice made me apprehensive. "His name is Ronnie," I said, "and I really like him." It was a father-daughter moment and I began boasting about Ronnie, saying how smart he was, and that he was a football player and the captain of his team. I was hoping my dad would be impressed.

But instead, he asked, "Have you slept with him yet?" When he said this, my heart sank, and rage welled up in me.

"That's none of your business," I said.

There were tears in my eyes, which he ignored. "I was just curious." He continued, "So how do you get it on?"

My mother was listening, and as he said this, she came running through the kitchen door, right up to him and in his face, and said, "What kind of fucking man are you, you whore-chasing fuck?"

He turned around and fled with her following him, still screaming. When he was out the door, I went over and hugged her. "Everything is going to be all right," she said.

With tears running down my cheeks I asked her, "Why is he like that?"

She said, "He's just a fucking asshole." Then I went back to washing the dishes.

I had many funny and loving times with Ronnie. The hours we spent with his family and alone together were a kind of oasis for me. But the incident at the Motel 6 had affected me and changed the way I thought about us. It made me realize that we were still children. When Ronnie turned eighteen, he was able to go to a strip club with his buddies. Afterwards, he told me where he had been and it made me mad. But it also made me think again about how young Ronnie and I were, and how much there was to experience in life, and how we were just on the threshold of that. We were children in a world of adults and probably couldn't cross the threshold together. I had been thinking about this for a while and had come to the conclusion that it would be best for us to go our separate ways. We had had a teenage love, but I felt—for myself at least—that I needed to grow up and to do that, I needed to be on my own.

When I shared my feelings with Ronnie, he was very upset and asked me "Why?" His heart was broken and mine was too. We both cried and held each other, and pledged that we would contact each other if going our separate ways didn't work out and see if we could come together again. But something inside me knew that was never going to happen.

Home Sweet Nightmare

A N IDEA THAT HAD BEEN on my mind for a long time was that I wanted a home of my own. It was what being an adult meant to me. I didn't dwell on it at the time, but it also meant leaving the house that had brought me so much pain. I was eighteen and was working as a supermarket checker. I had also started a house cleaning business to supplement my income and began taking classes at an adult school where I learned skincare and makeup and got a certification. I was moving on from Ronnie too. One of my brothers' friends, Mike Novak, had begun paying attention to me. He was nine years older than I was and had been around our house, it seemed, forever, hanging out to party with my brothers and their friends. He had always been nice to me, but now he took note of the fact that I was no longer a little girl.

Everyone called him "Big Mike" because he was six-foot-two and weighed 190 pounds. His skin was a lovely olive color and his imposing presence was softened by a sweet smile which I found endearing. I was impressed that he had a regular job running a sheet metal shop and, by all accounts, was a hard worker. He was also very kind and giving. He would always stop by at Christmas and other holidays with candy and liquor to help us celebrate and when he did, his conversation was direct and reassuring. I enjoyed talking to him.

Early one evening when everyone was at our house partying, Mike said he had something to show me and asked if I would take a ride with him on his chopper. We got on the bike and rode off into the warm evening. When we reached a house that had a "For Sale" sign in the front yard, Mike stopped and we got off. Then he turned to me and said, "I was thinking of buying this house. I want to have a family with someone like you."

I answered reflexively, "Oh, that's so sweet of you." But inside I wondered whether he was serious or this was just part of the party atmosphere we had come from.

One important lesson I had learned was that things were not always what they seemed, making it wise to be cautious. But I also thought: "God. That's what I want in life. To build a home. To have a family." I also began to ask myself if people can change and whether it was possible that Mike was ready to settle down.

At our house, tensions were rising. Leslie had moved back with the two children she had as a teenager now approaching adolescence. She was on her second divorce and in constant conflict with her daughters. I felt my nieces needed space and gave them my room, moving all my belongings into a closet. Added to the turmoil created by the new family were the usual troubled waters among the adults in the house. Between my sisters fighting with each other over clothes and anything else they could think of and my drive-through parents squabbling about money and everything they could think of, I wanted to escape.

Mike was a frequent visitor now and would use the occasions to ask me to dinner and tell me about the house which he had now bought, and how much he liked me. I liked him too. He was hard-working and caring and I kept thinking about what he said about wanting a home and a family. The temptation to go with him soon became very inviting and I thought, "I'm going to open this door and give it a try."

We had talked about living together, but not about marriage. I wanted to see what a joint household would feel like first. I was still concerned about his drinking and party ways, but I agreed to move in with him. Although he had been living in the new house alone for months while he pressed me to join him, it was still hardly occupied—a sign I should have taken more notice of. There were unpacked boxes scattered about and the furniture amounted to a bed, a couch, and a chair. When I moved in, I brought some pictures with me, and set about making it a home. Mike got me an office job with one of his business friends who had a sheet metal shop and our life together assumed an air of normalcy.

There were good times between us, but even as we grew comfortable together, it began to be clear to me that Mike had not left his old ways behind. As the weekend approached, people would come over to the house to drink and party, an exhausting ritual that continued non-stop for days. I was not a party animal and parties were not what I thought of when I thought of a family and a home. Soon, the new house began to feel like the one I had left. I confronted Mike about this on more than a few occasions, pleading with him to have his parties in other locations. But my pleas never led to changes. As my frustrations grew, my complaints became more emotional. I would break down in tears and repeat, "I want a home, I want a home. A home," I explained to him, "is a safe place." But my words made no impression. Either he didn't understand what I was saying or didn't want to. Or just couldn't.

I began to think about leaving. I kept saying to myself, "I've got to get out." As I neared the breaking point, he came home one evening with a basket of fruit and other foods, and we had a romantic picnic in front of the fireplace and became intimate, forgetting to use birth control. A month later, I began throwing up. It felt like the flu, but when it didn't let up, it dawned on me that I could be pregnant. I went to my doctor, who confirmed it. My immediate thought was: I cannot go through with this pregnancy; I need to get my life in order before I have children. So, when my doctor congratulated me, I said "Oh, no. I'm not going to go through with it."

He put his head down and said "Oh, I'm so sorry," and gave me the address of an abortion clinic.

But as soon as I got into my car, I started crying. I sat there for over an hour, feeling like I had been hit on the head.

I was depressed by the thought of losing my child and also by the prospect of raising it in the household I was in. When the storm passed, it left me drained, but also with a new resolve. It was as though, in the midst of this turmoil, I had been visited by an angel who told me to go through with the birth. The angel said, "Christine, it's going to be hard, but you can do it. This is a gift. You can raise this child."

I repeated to myself, "I can do this; I can do it on my own. I am going to raise this child and give it a better life than I had."

I drove home and didn't say anything to Mike. The next day, I went to the old house to see my mother, who had continued her visits. In a dysfunctional family, you keep the dance going and we did. Despite all that had transpired between us, she was still my mother, and when I needed counsel I instinctively turned to her. When I told her I was pregnant, she asked me what I was going to do. I said, "I'm going to keep this baby. I'm committed to it and I'm going to make sure this baby is going to get everything it needs." I had known I was pregnant for a few days, but still hadn't told Mike. When my mother heard this, she said, "You've got to tell him."

Mike was leaving that day for his parents' desert property to meet up with his friends and party. Gigi and I went over to the house where he was just loading the car. With my mother next to me, I said, "I've got to tell you why I've been so sick. I'm pregnant." Since he was already half way out the door, I said, "Let's talk about this when you come back." When he came back a few days later, he got down on his knees and sang Paul Anka's song "You're Having My Baby."

I was touched by his gesture, but wary. "I'm happy you feel this way," I said, "because I was planning on keeping the baby." Although things were not good between us, I believed he would be there for our child. More importantly, I was no longer focused on Mike and me. I was twenty-four years old, and my life had found a new center.

During the pregnancy, I was violently sick and had to quit my job, and could no longer make contributions to the household bills. I had to concentrate on my health and preparing for the new arrival. I was throwing up all the time. An unusual smell could trigger it. I even threw up over a glass of water. It got so I was afraid of food and had to see my doctor. He told me I was dehydrated and sent me to the hospital where I was given IV fluids.

The one comfort I had was my mom, who came over regularly to massage my back. I would lie down on my bed and she would rub my back and we would talk about babies. She talked about what it was like being pregnant with me and with my siblings. She told me she loved all her children. We talked about her breakdown. She said she never thought she would have a breakdown because she had felt strong for most of her life until it happened. "I always had to be such a strong person, but I guess there's just so much you can take." Our talks and the massages were a tonic to me. I felt cocooned by her. In those moments I felt that I had my mommy back.

While I was going through the ordeal of the pregnancy, I noticed that Mike was partying more and coming home less. There were many nights he was gone and I had no idea where. I began to get nervous that I would be alone when I went into labor and then after the birth, so I called my mother, who asked if I was as scared as I sounded. When I told her I was, she said she would come down and stay with me for two weeks around the due date. I was moved by this offer. It was a support I badly needed and I was grateful to be bonding with her again.

Towards midnight, on February 6, 1986, I went into labor. My water broke around ten the next morning and I called Mike at work to come and take me to the hospital. My mother stayed at the house to take care of my dogs and cats. At 11:45 a.m., I delivered a baby son, whom we named Michael Jr. and Big Mike went home to sleep.

I was so excited I counted my baby's fingers and toes to make sure they were all there. I kissed him, and held him, and gave him a breast. Though I was physically exhausted, a host of new feelings gave me energy. I had never felt such deep and overwhelming love for anyone. I could die for him without giving it a second thought. And I knew there wasn't anything I would not do to give my son a life that would be nothing like mine.

I stayed in the hospital overnight. At nine in the morning, the nurses told me I should get ready to go home with my baby. But when I phoned Big Mike at the house, there was no answer. I called my mother, who told me that he had never come home from the hospital. I called his work, but he was not there. I was beside myself. How would I get home?

While I was wondering about this, Henry came into my hospital room, which shocked me. I thought to myself: Is this for real? As he entered the room, he said "Congratulations, Christine." I immediately felt guilty that he had put himself out for me, although I should have thought: Yes, this is what fathers are supposed to do. Or maybe: What is he up to?

The nurse put a smock on him and he held little Michael for a while. While I was trying to get used to this person, he said, "What a really pretty baby, Christine." It turned my head. Ten years ago, I had vowed I would never ask him for help again after his refusal to pick me up at the supermarket. But now with Big Mike missing, and my son in his arms, I did. "I'm scared," I said. "I can't find Mike and have no one to take us home. Would you do it?" He immediately said he would. Five minutes later, Mike walked in, looking disheveled and tired. I was so relieved he had shown up, I didn't ask where he had been.

We drove home, stopping along the way to pick up some sandwiches since it was the noon hour. We were all sitting in the living room with the new baby, eating the sandwiches when there was a knock at the door. It was my mother's boyfriend, Clark. Not long afterwards, Mike's brothers showed up, bringing a twelve-pack of beer and some cigars. I excused myself and went to my bedroom to feed the baby, where I fell asleep for a half hour. When I woke, I heard music and went back into the living room. I was in my bathrobe. More people had arrived, and they were drinking and laughing. A party was underway, but it was not a party to welcome my baby into the world. It was more like an adult party to get away from the world, and—I couldn't help thinking—to get away from me and my baby.

The baby was crying and I took him back into the bedroom, where my mother helped me change him and put Vaseline on his rash. I started to cry. "I can't believe this," I said. "It's turned into another party."

She tried to comfort me and said, "I'm going to have a talk with him. Just stay here." She came back almost immediately. Mike was with her in an inebriated state. She looked at him sternly and said, "Mike, Christine just had your baby. We need to calm this down immediately." Mike looked at his son and he looked at me, and then he went back to the living room and told everyone to go home. Most of them did, but my sister Katie and her husband and Clark stayed and continued to get high. The three of them remained for the next two days, getting high and wandering around the house in a dazed state.

My mother and I were the only sober people in the house. I was too drained and feeling too vulnerable to throw the partiers out, but I thought to myself: This cannot continue. Either Mike is going to build a home for my child and me or I am going to do it without him.

Over the next months, I did my best to get Mike to behave as though he was committed to making us a home life. At times, when there were enough tears, he would stay and take care of things around the house. But these occasions were infrequent—no more than once a month or every two months—and my hopes that my home would come together remained unfulfilled. Mike did have a responsible side and made sure there was food in the refrigerator. When I needed things for the baby, we would go out together and get them.

But like clockwork, every Thursday evening, he would disappear and I would not see him again until Sunday.

By now, I knew that Mike wasn't going to change his ways, that he simply couldn't. I also had concluded that the life I had with him was not a life I wanted or was going to put up with. He was too attached to his work and his partying. For some reason, probably having to do with his own childhood and upbringing, he couldn't focus on family life. It was not that he didn't love me. Through the years after our life together was over, I saw that he did. He just couldn't shake off the habits that had become his life and be the partner and co-parent that I wanted. I couldn't go on like this. I wouldn't.

One evening, we were having a fight with little Michael in the room when I turned to him and said, "We have to stop this. We can't do this anymore. *I* can't do this anymore." When I said this, Big Mike stopped and a sober look crossed his face for a moment, as he took in the distressed look on his son's face. Then, without saying a word, he retreated into the bedroom. For an entire week, he made his presence scarce, staying away a lot at work. In the hours I spent alone in the house, I thought about my own childhood, about the days and nights and weeks I watched my mother drink herself into an angry stupor waiting for my father to come home, the rage building inside her. It scared me all over again, this time for my son. At the end of the week, when Big Mike and I finally had a moment alone, I said to him, "We really need to talk. We need to break up. I don't want my son to have the life I did."

Big Mike was sitting on the couch when I said this. He put his hand on his forehead and began to cry. To see this man break down was hard and brought up conflicting emotions. But it did not shake my resolve. We needed to separate. There was no going back from that. Mike was very good and responsible about it. He said he would move out and let Michael Jr. and me live in the house, and when he left, he was good about providing some support for us. He did care about his son and me. At least I had been right about that.

Changes

A FEW MONTHS BEFORE Michael's birth, my mother told me that her boyfriend Clark was cheating on her. I asked her why she put up with men who cheated on her. She said, "Everybody cheats, Christine. That's just called life." I didn't want to believe that, though I understood how it might look that way to her. It seemed to me just an excuse to avoid responsibility for the choices she made.

Our relations had begun to change when I moved in with Big Mike and especially after the birth of my son. She began to respect me more as a woman, which allowed us to exchange confidences that would not have been possible before. One day, she came to me and said, "I think this is the end of Clark and me. The other night when we were in bed, a drunken woman was outside the house screaming, 'Leave her, Clark. Come home with me.'" She said she always knew such a day would come because of their age difference. Then she said, "I would like to come and stay with you because I don't want to feel lonely in that big house. I'll help you with the baby."

I had always kept a piece of my heart open to my mother, hoping that she would return. Her offer made me very happy and I immediately accepted. There was an extra room in the house, and it became hers. It was the first time in twelve years we were together like that—a family—the first time since she had her breakdown and went from the hospital to live in Clark's mansion.

During the time my mother and I were bonding, Henry disappeared and was away for a long time, no doubt with his other women and, as I had come to realize, his other "families." I never knew the status of his relationships or how many homes he had bought to house them. I think he avoided marrying any of them, although he took Gigi to Mexico once and staged a "wedding" that could not be legally enforced. His other life was something I put to the side and tried not to think about. Becoming a mother had worked changes in my relationship to him too, but they were mainly changes in the way I saw him. I thought of them as reality checks to keep my emotions from running away with me and giving rise to hopes that were never going to come to fruition. It was a matter of not opening my heart to have it stepped on again. But once again the changes were not complete and I continued to suffer relapses. When he appeared at my bedside in the hospital, I was sucked into the old illusions. I was so happy he came, I convinced myself that the connection was real.

By this time, the absurdity of such feelings should have been ingrained in me. There were so many incidents that told me so. When I was fifteen, he took Janie and me to see his girlfriend Marge and her daughter. Marge was black, a fact that made him think well of himself. Henry's self-image was always that of a superior person, proud of the fact that he had progressive views. He had bought a four-garage, five-bedroom house for Marge and her two daughters in the richer neighborhood next to ours. It had a tennis court and swimming pool and was a far more spacious residence than the three-bedroom, one-bathroom home he had provided for my mother and her eight children.

While we were all in the car coming back from this visit, he turned to Janie and said out of the blue, "Marge told me she really liked you."

When he didn't say anything else, I asked him, "Did she like me?"

He answered my question without turning his head. "She didn't think much of you. In fact, she thought you'd grow up to be nothing." I started to cry; the pain of this jab stayed with me long afterwards. He always was able to find ways to hurt me and I was too young, or, for whatever reason, unable to fight back.

It was something of a miracle—or perhaps a sickness— that any part of me should have remained open for so long to the fantasy that he cared whether I lived or died. I had the scars of so many wounds that should have long ago closed the door to such childish illusions. The most constant and frequent of his put-downs were casual remarks to suggest I was illegitimate. Without any preamble or follow-through, he would say to me, "Do you know *who* you are? Do you know *what* you are?"

Despite the wounds these taunts inflicted, I always found myself coming back to the fact that he was my "father," the only one I had. So, I closed my eyes again and again to the fact staring me in the face—that I never really had a chance with him. Except, perhaps, in a perversely sexual way.

After Michael was born, I resumed my workouts and went almost daily to the gym, where I particularly liked the Jazzercise routines. One day when I was visiting the old house where my mother now lived, Henry asked me if I would like to go to the gym with him. I said yes, and we walked out the door. Then he said, "But you have to do me a favor. You have to act like my girlfriend, and we'll walk in arm in arm."

I said, "*What?*" and immediately began to cry. "No. I'm not going to do that." I went back to the front door to tell Gigi. "I can't believe this. He asked me to go the gym with him and I was excited to do it, but then he asked me to act like his girlfriend."

Gigi bolted out the door and yelled at him as he was walking away. "What the hell's wrong with you?"

In a familiar gesture of dismissal, he threw back "You two are crazy," and took off in his car.

Then a day came when I finally struck back. My mother often babysat little Michael at the old house, which she liked to visit and fix up, although no one was really living there since Henry was away so much. One day, I went over to get Michael, who was two and a half at the time. When I came in, he was sitting on the floor and my mother was watching him from the loveseat in our living room. I was a little startled to see Henry there too. He had recently learned to fly and was wearing his cap with pilot's wings and the name of the flight school he had attended on the brim. It was a family scene and I wanted to keep it that way, so I said in a friendly voice, "Well, how's it going with you?" When he didn't answer, I repeated myself. "How are you doing?"

I knew something bad was about to come my way when he pursed his lips in that patronizing smirk I knew so well. "You know," he said, "I've always wanted to ask you,"—as though he hadn't a million times before—"do you know even *who* you are? Or *what* you are?" He had that disgusting look on his face, and his voice had a steely edge as he delivered these familiar barbs. I felt the blood rush to my head, as I unexpectedly went right at him and asked what he meant. "Well," he said, punctuating the question with a sarcastic laugh, "Do you know who you *really* are?"

No one in the room, least of all me, was prepared for what happened next. "I know I'm not *you*," I replied. "I know I'm not going to be like you. You are a fucking cheater and a liar. You hurt me as a child when I couldn't defend myself. You hurt me like I will never hurt my own child. You abused me like I will never abuse him. You lied to me like I will never lie to him. I will never tell him he's nothing like you told me. I will never make sexual passes at him like you made passes at me. I don't know who you think *you* are, but the only thing you taught me as a parent is what *not* to be as a parent. I thank you for that. I will never forgive you for the pain you put me and our family through, so much pain that it's a wonder any of us can even think straight. You are a model of what *not* to be. Who the fuck do you think *you* are? Do you even *know* who you are?"

As the words left my mouth, Henry's jaw dropped as if he had been struck. My mother was sitting horrified on the loveseat in a clenched position. She was in tears. I was in a state of shock myself. I had no idea how I had done it, but I had. I had thrown a lifetime of abuse in his face. A deadening silence enveloped the room. I bent over and scooped up Michael and put him in the car. When the door closed, I started to cry, thinking all the while: I can't break down like this in front of my son. But he reached up and started kissing my face, saying, "Don't cry, mommy, don't cry." And then, "I know who you are, mommy, I know who you are. You're pretty, mommy. You're smart. I love you."

The tears were streaming down my face. "I love you too, baby. I love you and I will never hurt you," I said, and hugged him.

"I know, mommy," he responded. "I know."

The next time I saw my mother, I confronted her with the question that had been on my mind for a long time. I had even put it to her before but never got a response. I sensed now, however, that my outburst might have changed things. So, I asked her, "Why is Henry so mean to me? Why do I always feel like an outsider, and not one of his children?"

She was silent for a moment and pursed her lips while she weighed the answer. "He doesn't feel like you're his kid," she said. Then she took a breath, and asked me if I remembered the "Copper Digger," a neighborhood bar with live music entertainment. "I used to go there when Henry was away. I had a couple of different boyfriends whom I met there. On one of those occasions, I got pregnant. I think the father was one of the jazz musicians, but I can't be sure. What I am sure of is that it wasn't Henry. He wasn't around. That child was you."

Suddenly, it all made sense. I was not one of Henry's biological children. Instead, I was one of my mother's thoughtless revenges, conceived in a one-night stand with a man I would never know. This solved the mystery of Henry's anger, but I would never understand how he could hold onto his resentment for so long or take it out on a child who was innocent of the deed that had angered him.

My mother's decision to finally share this family secret after so many years of denial was one of a series of circumstances that made it possible for us to be closer than we had been since her breakdown. Her romance with Clark had broken Henry's hold so that his escapades no longer seemed to bother her. Now, Clark was gone and she was sober for the first time since I knew her.

Her sobriety was good news for us but had come late for her. She was fifty years old, but her body was already broken like that of an old woman. The kidney and liver problems that plagued her due to her diabetes and years of alcohol abuse had gotten so bad that the doctors had warned her that if she didn't stop, they would kill her. She did stop, cold turkey. I admired the strength she showed in doing that. It showed me again how strong-willed she was; but it also made me mad that she hadn't done this years before when we were all growing up and in her care.

A sign of her liberation from Henry was the reaction she had to his announcement that he had made "a new friend," as he put it, on one of his trips to Thailand. "Her name is Lennie," he told her. "She's a madam and she runs a brothel." Brazenness was a second nature to Henry and he presented Lennie's case as though it were a rescue mission. "She wanted to get out of there," he told Gigi, "so I'm bringing her over here with her two little daughters."

When my mother told me the story without emotion, I knew that she wasn't in love with him anymore. "I'm so sad for Lennie and her daughters," she told me. I thought she meant Henry would cheat on this family too. It would take many years, and a series of revelations from my sister, Melanie, before I would finally learn the much more terrible truth.

Despite my mother's newfound independence and calm, past traumas continued to haunt her. One day, I was visiting her at the old house and we were talking in the kitchen, when we heard the mailman at the front door. She was washing dishes and asked me if I could get the mail. There was an envelope from her sister, Nancy, and she eagerly opened it and started reading. But almost at once she started to cry, and cry so hard that she was shaking, and tears were flooding her cheeks. "What's wrong, mom?" I asked anxiously.

She struggled to catch her breath and said, "My sister sent me the little card we made for the funeral when my baby Timmy died. It's a little poem."

I asked her to read it to me, but instantly regretted doing so when she broke down, it seemed after, every line. "You don't have to finish it," I pleaded. But she wanted to and continued.

The poem was "Little Boy Blue" by Eugene Field. It was about a room full of toys waiting for the boy who once played with them to come back. It ended with this stanza:

And they wonder, as waiting these long years through
In the dust of that little chair,
What has become of our Little Boy Blue
Since he kissed them and put them there.

By the time she made it through these lines, she was soaked in tears. Then she said, "The pain never goes away."

My grandmother, Leoti, was a frequent visitor to the house. She and Gigi would cook and reminisce together and sometimes revisit old wounds. One day, I came over when the two of them were there. The house was very still and my grandmother was sunk into a living room chair looking very sad. I said, "Hey, grandma, what's going on?" but she didn't answer. My mother was in the kitchen and I asked her the same question and got the same non-answer. I could see they had been having a fight and guessed that Gigi had exploded on her mother. Neither of them wanted to talk. I said to my mom, "Why are you fighting with grandma? She looks so sad out there. She's old, mom. Can't you stop this?"

But all my mother would say to me was, "She knows what she's done."

Later on, when my grandmother left, I was able to talk to my mother about what had happened. She began by saying,

"Hey, listen. Your grandma is not such a perfect grandma." Then she told me what their fight was about. It was over the way my grandmother had abandoned her more than forty years before. She was all of thirteen and Leoti had left her along with her sisters in the house with my grandfather, the violent drunk and sexual predator who had killed her horse, Rosie. Her life under his roof was miserable and finally so miserable that she ran away and went to live in an abandoned car.

One night, it was raining and cold and she was feeling lonely and abandoned, desperately wanting her mother. "I've got to go and find my mom," she said to herself. "I'm in a really bad way."

She got out of the car she had been living in and went over to the house where her grandmother lived and where she was sure her mother had gone. When she got to the house, her grandmother was sitting on the porch, smoking her corn cob pipe. She was a dark, forbidding woman with a stern disposition, and a long black braid of hair now streaked with gray that went down to her waist. "I was afraid of her," my mother confessed.

She went up to the porch and told her grandmother that she was looking for her momma and asked where she was. But all the old lady said was, "You're better not knowing."

Cotton Top pleaded. "I know she's in this house." But her grandmother continued to puff on the pipe and would not answer. The hurt that little Cotton Top was feeling was terrible. "I hated her then," she said to me.

When my mother related this incident to me I thought, "My God, you did the same thing to me. That is just the way

I felt." But now that I was on my own and a mother myself and my mom was so obviously hurting and vulnerable, my heart just went out to her—to the little girl Cotton Top—and I opened my arms and hugged her.

Gigi never found it in her heart to forgive her mother. As Leoti approached the end, they moved her to Stockton. But Gigi pulled away, and never went to see her. As with me, she took her grievance to the grave.

After separating from Big Mike, I had gone back to work. With the certificate I received from the cosmetics school, I began doing make-up for weddings and photograph sessions. The income from this work provided us with some support. But, I needed a regular job, which I was able to secure doing make-up and skin care in a Santa Monica dermatologist's office. To take the job, I needed help from my mother since I couldn't leave Michael alone or hire someone to look after him. Luckily, the changes she had gone through finally made it possible for her to be there for me. I was able to take the job because she was willing to babysit full-time for my child while I was away. It was the completion of a circle that had been broken long ago. She was a good grandmother to Michael. An avid reader herself, she took time to read books to him. They played games and watched TV shows together. Above all, she gave him love and didn't withdraw it suddenly or abandon him as she had her own children. She did for him what she should have done for us whose lives would have been a lot different if she had.

We still had occasional moments triggered by the legacies of the past. Sometimes it was the past in me that accounted for the explosion. One evening when I came home from work, I put a little dinner together. My mother wasn't feeling well and went into the back room with Michael to lie down. I made hot cocoa and brought it to them. I could see my mother was enjoying it, when all of sudden, she said in a pleading, child-like voice that was almost a whisper, "I want you to be my mommy."

As soon as she said it, something snapped in me. The rage from all the years of my childhood erupted. I had no control over the feelings or what I said to her. "I wanted you to be *my* mother," I screamed back. "And what did I get? *Nothing.*"

Heart pounding, I bolted out of the room. I was shocked by what I had said and immediately felt guilty. The voice I had just heard was the ghost of Cotton Top, who had been abandoned like me and left to fend for herself in the cold and the rain. When I was able to recover, I went back and told her I was sorry and that I loved her. I gave her a hug, and we never discussed it again.

One evening, Janie came over. She was about five months pregnant and I was looking forward to the arrival of a new cousin for Michael. But I could see Janie was depressed. She began complaining about her husband: "He doesn't pay attention to me. After work, he goes off to party. I'm pregnant and I can't party. I don't know how to get him to pay attention to me."

I could see that my mother had little patience for Janie's complaints because she had little patience for Janie's husband and the by-now familiar stories about his drinking and partying. My mom and I were sitting on the bed in her bedroom. She leaned back against the pillows, arched her left eyebrow and in a sarcastic voice said, "You want to know how to get his attention? You want to know how to please a man? Go home, suck his dick, and make him something good to eat."

Janie was hurt by this response and said, "What? What the hell, mom? Why would you say that?"

My mother rose from the bed and disappeared into the bathroom saying, "I'm sick of this. You figure it out."

In moments like these, I got to see how distressed my mom was about the choices her daughters had made and how their lives were turning out. The one who had fared best was Henry's oldest child, Helen, who had been the first to leave. She was out the door when she turned eighteen and never looked back. She went to college, became a high school teacher of French, and then married a military man who eventually became a general and worked in the Pentagon. She never had children and, except for one short visit that she and her husband made to my mom, she never had contact with us. I always wondered how great a role this distance played in her ability to lead a healthy life.

Katie, who was next to oldest of the girls, was not so fortunate. Even as a teenager, she was hostile towards Gigi and hardly spoke to her. Probably the humiliation of the infamous parent-teacher night and similar episodes were responsible. Katie was a beauty and well-spoken. She was also one of those people where everything was about her. She once gave me a blouse and took it back, saying, "It'll look better on me," which instantly turned the gift into a weapon.

She was so pretty she could have married anybody, but when she was eighteen, she left the house to go live with a shiftless construction worker in his parents' basement. He was a "loadie" like the ones I avoided as a teenager. Both of them were routinely high on pot, then cocaine and meth.

When Katie gave birth to a daughter, she cleaned up for a while, but then she went back and became a serious addict, living on welfare in "Section 8" government housing, earmarked for the poor. When her daughter was in her teens, she became pregnant by a local gang banger who went to prison for attempted murder. My mother had stopped talking to Katie and the rest of the family eventually avoided contact, not only because she was constantly hitting them up for drug money, but because it was too dangerous to know her and her daughter. The last one to cut her off was Melanie, who regularly signed over her own paycheck to her until she realized it was all going to feed Katie's addiction. When Melanie finally ended her charity payments, Katie reacted as though she was the injured one. She told Melanie, "Go fuck yourself," and refused to speak to her anymore.

The daughter whose troubles were most on my mother's mind now was my older sister, Leslie. She had entered her teens in the sixties, was always bra-less, and aggressively promiscuous. At sixteen, she became pregnant and left our home to marry a Hell's Angels biker. After she bore him a second daughter, he emerged as a full-blown reprobate—a lazy alcoholic, who "came out" as a cross-dressing homosexual, abandoned their household, and refused to support the children he had fathered. Her next husband, Marvin, was an accomplished computer programmer, a stable and kind person who quickly bored her. She began seeing other men and eventually divorced him. When the marriage fell apart, Marvin called and asked to see me. He told me how he missed Leslie and his daughters and how alone he had felt in the marriage. Then he said, "Your sister is a cold woman."

How cold, we soon learned, when Leslie moved into an apartment with the man who became her third husband, an alcoholic like the first. The small space of the apartment made her daughters, then twelve and thirteen, an inconvenience to the newlyweds, so she threw them out of her house to fend for themselves. She also did it to collect the welfare checks and food stamps earmarked for them and use the money for herself. When my mother and I became aware of what she had done, we went looking for the girls. Eventually, the older one called me and said, "Aunt Christine, I'm hungry and scared."

I was relieved to hear her voice, and said, "You tell me right now where you are, and grandma and I will come to get you." We did just that, and my mother put my niece up in her house. Soon afterwards, we found the younger girl in Whittier, living on the open porch of a friend.

My mom took both girls in and we were going to get them back in school. But first we had to deal with Leslie, since she was their mother. My sister's heartlessness was something I could never understand. Even when my mother abandoned us to run off with Clark, it came only in the wake of a mental breakdown. Leslie had no such excuse. When I called to tell her that we had found her daughters and were going to get them back in school, she flew off the handle. "You fucking bitch. Who the fuck do you think you are?" she said. "It's none of your fucking business." I told her I wasn't going to let my nieces become homeless, but all she thought about was protecting herself, which meant keeping what she had done from the eyes of others.

My mother, who was listening to my end of the conversation, took the phone from me and said, "Leslie, you're a fucking asshole. This is horrible. It's against the law. These two girls need a mother."

Hearing this, I thought, "*Finally*, my mother has become the reasonable one."

The rest of the family responded in similar fashion. When Tommy came by Gigi's house, found Leslie's kids there, and was told what happened, his reaction was one of utter disgust. "Leslie's just about Leslie," he said, "she's a bitch." In a matter of days, Leslie's new husband called and was more sensible about the problem. He had probably warned her about the consequences if child services found out what she had done because soon Leslie was singing a different tune, but not really thinking in a different way.

She came over with some pictures of her daughters and said to me, "These girls have let me down so badly. I was such a good mother. How could they have done this to me?" This response should have shocked me, but it was so much the person I knew–the one who turned reality upside-down to make herself the victim—that it didn't. To avoid the potential problem with the law, she called the parents of the girls' biker father, who was then living in San Diego, and got them to have his sister take the girls in.

The sister was also an alcoholic and in her household the girls slid steadily downhill. The younger of the two became a meth addict. As a child, her older sister had been a loving, gregarious individual, intelligent and ambitious. Everyone who knew her could see she had a lot of potential. But now, she turned her talents to more destructive ends. She became the leader of a drug gang in the San Diego area, robbing houses and running a meth lab. Eventually, she was caught and sentenced to eight years in prison for her crimes. My mother was heartbroken. "I knew my daughter would fuck those girls up," she said when I told her the news.

Leslie's behavior was so alien to me that it was hard to think of her as my sister. How could she be so callous to her own children? How could she be so selfish? Much as I welcomed my mother's response, it was also unnerving. Here she was, condemning a behavior that had characterized much of her own motherhood. She even attacked the way Leslie dressed—the way she was always bra-less and seductive— which was inappropriate for a mother with small children, but obviously inspired by the model set by the critic herself.

My mother's unexpected reactions revealed a new side of her, and possibly regret for the way she had raised us. Thinking about what had happened made me wonder about a divide I had always been aware of that had begun to seem like a chasm I could not cross. I had always felt like an outsider in the family as though I had been born to follow a different set of rules than its other members. It wasn't that I judged them for being different—although when Leslie threw away her children, I could not help but be repelled. It was more that it wasn't in me to do what they did—to mimic their reckless behaviors, ill-conceived attachments and cold-hearted rejections. I did not have the anger in me that would cause me to do such things. Nor could I understand how they did not see that their actions might come back to haunt them.

While I felt like an outsider, I desperately wanted not to be. I wanted to be in and of the family. I wanted to be connected to them despite our differences because these were the people who had shared the life that had made me what I was. They were the only "home" I knew. The fact that my mother now saw Leslie's selfishness the way I did, encouraged my fantasy of belonging. It was my own form of recklessness. If I had not been so bent on bringing the family together I might have saved myself a world of hurt and foreseen that a day would come when the demons it housed would blow us all apart.

Marriage and a Visit

WITH MY MOTHER THERE to help, I was comfortable living alone with my son. The three of us formed a kind of household, although my mother was staying in the old residence a few blocks away. She was constantly over to my house and I to hers and our joint mission to raise Michael brought us closer than we had ever been.

My new job with the dermatologist was a welcome contrast to the turmoil with which I was familiar. I found the order and calm of the office reassuring. The drive time to work was over an hour, and with the eight hours I had to spend on the job I had very little personal life. When Michael was four, I enrolled him in a Montessori school. My son was a reader like my mother and was fascinated by a science book I bought for him, along with a little lunch pail with Ninja turtles. It turned out to be the first sign of the career he would eventually pursue. Before school started, I got him a Buster

Brown haircut and thought he looked so cute in the new cut with his big brown eyes and pink lips. On the first day, I drove him to school and took pictures. Since he was shy, I hung around a little to see how he was doing. When I had to say goodbye, I cried. But I was also happy thinking: My son is on his way.

While I was pretty satisfied with my situation and didn't see how I could squeeze much more into my days, people were constantly pushing me to go out on dates and men were calling. A lot of them were wealthy and knew about me because of my work and the networks connected to it. I accepted a few invitations but soon discovered that the men who asked me out were only interested in having what they thought was a good-looking woman on their arm or a casual fling. As a result, the invitations didn't result in any serious engagements. Since I quickly saw that they weren't going to lead to the kind of home that I still longed for, the few relationships I began didn't last very long.

One of my new acquaintances was a famous Beverly Hills realtor named Elaine Young whose clients included Elvis Presley and Frank Sinatra. Elaine was a glamorous blonde who had been married six times and drove around in a Rolls Royce with the license plate "Elaine 7." She had received a certain notoriety after the largest realty firm in Los Angeles fired her for telling an AP reporter that she would sleep with a client to close a deal. Ten years before I met her, a plastic surgeon had injected loose silicon into her face which migrated to her eye and other areas causing such problems that she became famous again as a poster girl for plastic surgeries gone wrong. Eventually, she came to the dermatologist for whom I worked to try to hide the irreparable damage that had been done.

Elaine and I struck up a relationship during the skin treatment sessions I gave her. One day, she asked me to go to a Hollywood premiere after work. I was reluctant and tried to beg off because I was very tired and also because I missed my son. But in the end, I went along with her. She was eager to impress me with some celebrities that evening which included Clint Eastwood and Charlton Heston, both of whom she knew. It was fun and a little exciting, but I was tired and thinking about my son. I soon discovered that I was one of several young women whom Elaine collected as an entourage and took to events like the premiere. Surrounding herself with attractive young women and introducing them to celebrities turned out to be a way she promoted her business.

The tiredness I was feeling was not just the result of work and my long commute to Santa Monica. It became such a problem that I went to see my doctor about it and he diagnosed me as having "chronic fatigue syndrome" caused by the Epstein-Barr virus. I conveyed this news to Elaine the next time she asked me to go out with her to another celebrity event. When I did so she said, "Oh my God. I have a writer friend who had Epstein-Barr for several years and found a doctor who has a cure. I want to give him your number. Maybe he can help you." I said okay and before I knew it, a man named Joel Stein was on the phone giving me advice. He called several times after that with suggestions about diet and acupuncture treatments, then offered to come see me.

That seemed a bit forward, hoping it would put him off, I told him I lived in Orange County. But he said he was scheduled to speak in Irvine in a couple of weeks and could come to see me then. The date was a Saturday and I was working in the doctor's Orange County office, so I gave him that address.

On the appointed day, Joel showed up, as he said he would. He was a short, somewhat stocky man in his early fifties, dressed in a yellowish silk jacket, pants to match, and the clumpiest white shoes I had ever seen. The first thing I thought to myself was: This man does not know how to dress. When the doorbell rang, I had to come out of the inner office and let him into the waiting room. As I did so, the office door shut behind me and I realized I had left the keys inside and locked myself out. I began to panic, but when I explained to him what had happened, he just opened one of the windows that surround the inner office and started to climb through it. When he got inside, he went to the door and opened it for me. I was impressed.

I was feeling pretty ill that day, but I showed him around the office and let him look at some of the before-and-after photos of the doctor's patients. After a prolonged silence he said, "I don't know. I find this all so weird." I thought: Well that's not the best foot forward on your first encounter. I thought it was pretty snobbish, in fact, and I took it as a put-down of what I did. As if sensing the awkwardness of the silence that followed, he began nervously thumbing through the three or four books about Epstein-Barr he had brought and singling out passages to read to me. He was so nervous and I was feeling so uncomfortable, I didn't know whether to terminate the meeting then and there, or stick it out. While I was debating this, he asked me, "Where are we going to dinner?"

I was not prepared for that. "I didn't know we were going to dinner," I replied.

At that point, all I was thinking was: I want to end this, pick up my son, and go to bed. He looked really crestfallen as I told him I really wasn't feeling well and had to go home. But disappointed as he was, he was very nice as we said goodbye. By the time I arrived home, put down my purse, kicked off my shoes, and gave my son something to eat, there were three messages from him on my phone. The first said, "Oh, by the way, you should really read this page and chapter," and "There's another book coming out that I will get for you." Then the beep and another message, "Oh and here's another passage you should read…" Then another beep and, "I hope I'm not bothering you, but I really liked meeting you and I hope you will get some benefit out of the books," and "What about going to dinner with me when you feel better?"

Another couple of months would pass before I accepted his invitation. During the wait, he would call to find out how I was and whether the advice was helping me. There was definitely something about him that was attractive. There was the fact that he was concerned about me, but even more that he never gave up. He was persistent but in a kind and respectful way and I liked that.

When we finally had the dinner, it was off Wilshire Boulevard in Santa Monica at Hamburger Hamlet, a restaurant chain in the building where our office was. It was a pleasant dinner and we talked a lot, although I was guarded about my private life, as I usually was. He told me that he had written a book that was a number one *New York Times* bestseller. He also said that he was the head of an organization that was somewhat political. He tried to explain to me what that meant and what he did, but since I wasn't political and wasn't familiar with the issues and personalities he mentioned, what he was saying didn't make much sense to me.

What really got my attention, as our dates continued, was the way he provided a security for me in our relationship that I realized I desperately needed. Around him, things seemed normal and safe. Other men I dated had just wanted to touch and fondle me and have sex. When I resisted or didn't give them what they wanted, they would turn on me angrily, as though I had deprived them of something they were owed. In contrast, Joel genuinely cared for me and would never think of forcing himself on me or becoming violent when he didn't get his way. His love and concern for me made me feel safe and made me want to sleep with him early on.

As our relationship progressed, I discovered in Joel a very interesting person and a passionate one. I found myself looking forward to our visits. They were a welcome change from the years of uncomfortable and short-lived dates I had had until then. However, a problem did come up, which almost caused me to end our affair at the start. And I probably would have, if it had not been for my mother's counsel.

Joel was recently divorced and there were several incidents that made me feel he had not completely moved on from the marriage. I knew he had done radio interviews and

I said I would love to hear one of them. He gave me a tape and said I could take it home with me and bring it back. But when I played the tape, there was also a voice message he had recorded from his ex-wife, which he obviously didn't realize was on it. His ex-wife was very angry and was running down a laundry list of reasons why she should be. I didn't know what to make of it, but it disturbed me enough that I turned to my mother for advice.

"Mom," I said, "the weirdest thing happened. Joel gave me a tape and on the other side, was his ex-wife cussing him out and I don't know what to think." She listened to the tape. "Christine, honey," she said, "when women are going through divorce proceedings, they can come up with awful things to say. This woman sounds a little crazy and from your accounts, he sounds like a really nice person. Just watch his behavior and then make up your mind." It occurred to me that this was kind of amusing advice coming from her considering the men she had chosen in her life. Had she watched their behaviors, or altered her own because of them? But then maybe she had learned from all the times she didn't. In any case, she had been offering me much wiser advice now that she was sober, so I did what she said.

Over the next months, I felt more and more confident in Joel's affections for me while my own feelings for him were growing. I was encouraged to let these feelings go where they might because I saw that Joel did not do drugs, there was no alcohol in his refrigerator, and he was reliable in all things that mattered. Nonetheless, I held an important part of me back. There had been so much hurt in my life from broken relationships and I had witnessed so much damage to my siblings and their children from wrong choices they made that I decided to keep the fact that I had an eight-year-old son a secret until I knew Joel better. When we had a date, I would always travel to his condo in Marina del Rey rather than have him pick me up at my home in Orange County.

We had been seeing each other for more than four months when I decided to finally tell Joel about my son. I was very nervous about broaching the subject because I didn't know how he would react—either to the fact that I had a son or that I had kept his existence a secret. As it turned out, I needn't have worried. Joel had four grown children of his own and told me he not only understood that I needed to protect my son's feelings, but this gave him confidence that I would protect his. The next weekend, I brought Michael to meet Joel along with two of his cousins. We took them to the Air and Space Museum at the California Science Center. Bringing the cousins along made the whole occasion easier for Michael. The afternoon was filled with their boyish pranks and good humor with Joel joining in, all of which was a great relief to me.

While I was most comfortable taking things slowly and proceeding with caution, Joel was the opposite. Once he set his mind on something, there was no stopping him. No sooner had I introduced him to Michael and the boys than he announced he was moving into another condo in the Marina complex—this one with two bedrooms—and said he would like me and Michael to move in with him. This was way too fast for me. And besides, the environment was wrong. There were no families with children in the condo complex and I didn't even want to think about uprooting my son, who was still in the third grade. I said no. Despite his disappointment, Joel seemed to understand. He was soon using the empty extra room as a play area for Michael and his cousins. One day, he set about building them tents, which particularly warmed my heart. Here was a family man, who would take fatherhood seriously.

Although it went against his nature, Joel deferred to my timetable as best he could. Then, one day, he invited me to dinner at a restaurant in the Loews Hotel in Santa Monica, overlooking the ocean. There were orchids on our table. Still oblivious to what might be happening, I thought they were put there by the restaurant. Joel had a knowing smile on his face, but was looking unusually nervous as well. Before I could catch my breath, he presented me with a ring and asked me to marry him.

I blush to recall this moment more than twenty years later because I giggled and couldn't answer for what seemed like an eternity to him. I was completely unprepared for a proposal—and yet there was no reason I should have been. It wasn't Joel or the question he was asking. It was just that the idea of marriage was remote from my thinking. It didn't help that my mother had warned me, "Every man is going to hurt you." Or that the relationships I had been close to growing up had been so toxic and impermanent. I had just mentally pushed the whole idea off to the side until it was completely out of sight. I really hadn't thought about marriage to anyone, which was why I was drawing a blank. I knew I loved him and the answer to his question was always going to be yes, but he had to persist through several pauses and appeals before my head cleared so that I could give it to him. When I did so, it let all the nervous energy out of the air between us, and we had a romantic evening, while I was left to wonder where I was heading.

We were now formally engaged, but I still proceeded with caution. It took two more years before I agreed to a marriage date. First, I wanted to see what living under the same roof would be like. I told Joel that Michael and I were not going to move into the Marina, so we looked together for a house to buy and finally found one in the Pacific Palisades. The house we chose needed some fixing, but it was situated in a beautiful, upscale neighborhood, where my child would be safe.

The traumas of my childhood made me a tense person normally, but as the day approached for the move, my anxiety levels rose to new heights. I was thirty-five and had lived in roughly the same neighborhood all my life. With the move, my mother, siblings, and friends would be two hours away. Even more worrying was the impact the separation might have on my son. Would he be okay leaving his friends and school? How would he adjust to Joel being the new man of the house? To his new school? The anxiety caused by these questions led to panic attacks so severe that, at one point, I had to breathe into a brown bag to be able to breathe at all. But I knew I had to get control of the fear for the sake of my son and was able to do so.

Michael was nervous, too and at first didn't want us to move in. He liked Joel, but the strangeness of a new home scared him. Once we settled in, however, he adjusted and we enrolled him in the local elementary school. Joel helped him with his homework and encouraged him generally. He was very shy, so Joel would go to the local park with him and organize basketball games with other kids his age and encourage him to engage. In this, as in other aspects of our family life, having Joel's support was the element I had been missing and having it now made me very happy.

I called the new house the "Brown Box" because that's what it looked like. Joel assured me we could fix it up and we did. We put a new floor in the living room, had the kitchen re-modelled, built a new wooden staircase up to the second level, and bought stained glass windows with geometric designs which I didn't like. Joel had very different tastes from mine and did not always pick up the signs when I disagreed with his decisions. Perhaps I was not forceful enough as well.

After we had been living in the Palisades for two years, I finally agreed to tie the knot. As I had come to expect, although it always puzzled and distressed me, my family— with the exception of my mother—was not exactly supportive. My brother, Rick, told Big Mike that Joel would turn his son into a Jew and force him to wear a *yarmulke*. Big Mike came to me upset and said, "I don't want my son getting into religions that he knows nothing about." I told him nothing like that was happening and that my brother just wanted to cause trouble and get Joel upset with me. Janie and her husband took an interest in Joel's Jewishness as well, warning me that Jews were stingy and treated their wives like slaves. I told them they were ridiculous but was shocked to see how prejudiced they were. It bothered me that they should react so negatively to something so good that was coming into my life. I wanted them to be happy for me, as I would have been for them, but that wasn't going to happen. Perhaps because their own marriages were so troubled they were looking for signs that mine would be too.

Our marriage took place in June 1998 with over two hundred people attending the ceremony. Among them were three of my sisters and their husbands, two of my brothers and their wives, and Henry, who gave me away. We hired a bodyguard because I couldn't trust the alcoholics in my family not to make a scene. My mother couldn't handle crowds and didn't come, but I knew she was supportive and that was all that mattered. Joel was friends with Arianna Huffington, who graciously provided her elegant Brentwood home for the ceremony when our first venue fell through.

When my son came up to Arianna's bedroom where I was getting ready and I saw him all dressed in his little suit and tie and with his big hazel eyes, he was so adorable and I was so happy that I cried. Arianna was getting ready as well and in the quiet of her bedroom, where we were dressing and putting on our makeup, she told me how sad she felt because she was no longer married and was lonely. We were silent for a moment, then she got up and said, "Well it's time for me to put myself together and be a gracious hostess and for you to be married." We went downstairs to the ceremony, which was performed at the majestic entrance to her home by one of the six congressmen Joel had invited. The whole afternoon was overwhelming and I couldn't have asked for a more memorable celebration. I was deeply moved by the fact that my husband had given me something that I had never thought would be mine.

Looking back, I don't know why I let Henry give me away, except that it's something every girl wants her father to do. It was part of our family dysfunction to keep the surface normal even though nothing else was. It showed me I still had not freed myself from the family web, where we adjusted to realities that made no sense and hid them to keep up the illusion that we were a family when we were not.

While my mother was unable to make the wedding, she did come and stay with us in our home in the Palisades. She stayed for days and even weeks at a time. I enjoyed her company and the talks we had. She was always ready with a suggestion when I had questions about what to do with Michael or my husband. We continued these visits in the houses we lived in until she died. I was the only one of my sisters who took her in, an indication of how full of anger they were even though they were many years into adult-hood and had teenage children of their own. I had a hard time understanding this. My husband thought that the anger they held onto was related to the unhappiness in their lives. I half understood what he was saying. I had anger in me too, but I was not going to let it control my relationships or my life.

For the most part, my mother and I got along now, but occasionally the hurts of the past would surface and come between us until we were able to get hold of ourselves, calm down, and back off. These points of friction would usually occur when we talked about family matters and days gone by and she would try to lay the responsibility for whatever had happened on me. I would come back at her, "Really? You're the one who left me when I was fourteen." And the sparks would fly from there. But I always regretted these incidents and vowed to try to avoid them.

My mother was a great reader and liked Joel a lot. She made a scrapbook of his literary achievements and talked with pride about what he was doing. Although life had mellowed her, she was still troubled and beneath the surface was not at peace. Understanding this made me even more regretful about the times we fought.

One day when Joel was away on a speaking tour, she had a second breakdown, which disturbs me even now to recall. The day had started like any other. I noticed she was a little off and distant, but I thought nothing of it. Then, at some point, I was in the kitchen when I felt her staring at me from the couch in the living room, which was visible through the open doorway. My heart just dropped. It was the face I had seen when I was fourteen. The eyes were frenzied, the expression of someone possessed. Anxiously, I said to her, "Mom, Are you okay?" She screamed and made an animal-like sound in response and walked into the kitchen. My son, Michael, was standing there and I saw his bewilderment. She went over to one of the kitchen drawers and pulled out a knife.

I shouted to Michael, "Go upstairs and shut the door."

Then I asked her what she was doing with the knife. She screamed, "I want a knife," and began making those unearthly noises. Then she said, "The aliens can hear us."

When I heard that, I asked her if she was taking her meds. "For what?" she shot back. I knew then she had checked out and there was no reaching her. Still, I tried to talk her down. I asked her to give me the knife and said I would take care of it. At the same time, I thought, "Please God, don't let her stab me." I tried to reassure her, saying that I would take care of everything. She dropped her hand to her side and I went over to her and took the knife from her. Then she went back to screaming. Michael was at the top of the stairs calling me and asking if I was all right. I told him again to go to his room and lock the door. I asked my mom why she was upset. "The aliens can hear us," she repeated.

Then she erupted, flailing her arms and making animal sounds. She was shrieking like a wild bird: *Eeeeeeuh! Eeeeeeuh! The aliens.* But it was she who looked and sounded like an alien. I began to panic. I felt a rush of the same feelings of fear and abandoment I had as a child when I saw her lose her mind the first time. I reached for the phone and called Rick, who had comforted me then. I said "Mom has lost her mind again, "I can't control her. I'm scared. Please come."

But years of drug and alcohol abuse had changed Rick and brought out his cruel side. Instead of comfort he barked, "That's your problem, call the fucking cops," and hung up.

Meanwhile, my mother had run upstairs and was threatening to throw herself out of the window. I called 911 and begged them to come quickly. When they arrived, she pointed at them and screamed, "They're aliens!" One of the officers told me they would have to call a special unit to take her to a medical center and put her on a seventy-two hour hold. When the special unit came, they said they would have to cuff her. They asked her if she liked ice cream and when she said yes, told her they would give her all the ice cream she wanted if she put her hands behind her. I said to her, "You have to listen to them," and kissed her on the face. When she placed her hands at her back, they put the cuffs on. She was crying and it broke my heart. I held her face, which was hot with tears while I held back my own, so as not to alarm her. I was flooded with all the feelings I had as a child when they took her away.

When Joel returned from his speaking engagements, we went to the medical center to see her. I brought her a Paddington bear so she would have something to hold onto. She was sedated, but seemed to be coming back to normal. She said her sugar levels had been off and she was fine now, and begged me to get her out. A woman appeared who she said was her roommate. The woman looked to be in her twenties and was overweight. She said, "Your mom's really great. Your mom and I are the only sane ones here. My only problem is my father took a piece of his brain and put it in mine to control me, but I'm working to deal with it." My mom and I looked at each other and my mom said again, "Please get me out of here." Then the doctor came and we pleaded with him, he told us that we could secure my mother's release the next day.

I had already called Henry to tell him what happened and he said he would pick her up, which he and Rick did the following morning. When they got to the house they called me. Rick said, "Oh she's fine, why did you call the police on our mother. You got her locked up for nothing."

"You know very well why I called the police," I shouted back in exasperation. "You were on the phone listening to her screaming about the aliens. I asked you to help and you told me it was my problem and I should call the police." I hung up. I was so furious. It felt like I was never going to extricate myself from all the craziness, lies, and selfishness of my family.

The central focus of my life now was my son and his adjustment to his new environment. I paid particular attention to his education. I wanted him to have the opportunities I didn't due to the chaos of the environment I grew up in. My sense of loss over this deprivation would only grow with the years, and I was determined it was not going to be a regret shared by my son. Michael was now going to middle school in Brentwood. It was both a charter and magnet school, but was not without problems. In his first year as a sixth grader, a situation arose that made me feel I had failed to provide him with good advice previously. The year before at the public elementary school in the Palisades, he had to deal with a schoolyard bully. I had told him he should protect himself from bullies, but that there would never be a reason to hit a girl, even in self-defense. I advised him to just walk away if the occasion arose. But when he moved on to middle school, I had to face the fact that my advice was misguided and also that the public schools were not the best place to provide him with the education I wanted him to have.

In his first year at the middle school, an eighth-grade girl who outweighed him by fifty pounds demanded his lunch money and said she would beat him up if he didn't give it to her. He told me later that he was considering fighting back but remembered what I had told him. So instead, he gave up his money for a month, and had such anxiety he lost ten pounds. Because of his anxiety, his grades were suffering too. But when Joel and I went to the school principal to complain, he said, "Well, Mrs. Stein, maybe your son needs to learn that there are good neighborhoods and bad neighborhoods."

The principal was referring to the fact that the girl was black and, as a result of district policy, had been bussed from South Central to upscale Brentwood. His attitude was to adjust to a bad circumstance rather attempt to correct it. "Michael will have to walk through a different hallway to avoid her," he said.

I was shocked. "Are you kidding me? It's your job to keep your students safe." But there was no budging him. To make matters worse, as we were leaving his office, the girl came up to us and laughed at my son. I was furious. I had plenty of tough life experience to know that encouraging bad behavior was bad for all parties concerned. I was not going to let my son go undefended. "I know you think it's funny stealing money from younger and smaller kids," I said to the girl. "But if you do this again, I will come to school and take your lunch money, and you'll be lucky if that's all I do."

When we got back home, I apologized to Michael for instructing him not to hit back if the aggressor was a girl. "When it's someone who is bigger and bullying you," I said, "you need to defend yourself." Michael then told me he had seen the same girl and a group of her friends beat up a little black child in a wheelchair outside one of the school bathrooms and take his money. When he told me this, it just fueled my anger and prompted me to make an appointment with the vice principal, who was black, and in charge of school discipline. He was a nice man and very sympathetic, but what he said to me was that he had three thousand youngsters to look after and did not have the personnel to look after all of them. He advised me to enroll Michael in a martial arts class.

This was the last straw. I decided right then that I was going to move Michael out of the public school system. On the recommendation of a neighbor, I enrolled him at Calvary Christian, a local Lutheran school where the authorities had not abdicated their role as guardians and teachers and problems like this did not exist. Almost immediately on his transfer, Michael's grades began to improve.

This was not the only change I made at the time. In my own life, I seemed to be progressing in two-year segments and was ready to move again. Many things prompted my restlessness. I wanted a backyard, I thought our kitchen was too big, I was irritated by the geometric designs of the stained-glass windows that Joel had put in. It was only later, after two more moves, that it dawned on me that these were only pretexts. It wasn't the limitations of the houses that prompted my desire for change. What I wanted was change itself. I focused on my environment, but the problem was really me. I wanted change because something was missing in me that I couldn't identify or name. I had felt unsettled all my life, never sure of my place in the worlds I inhabited. It was Henry's accusation still haunting me—*Who do you think you are?* I didn't really know yet.

As my restlessness increased, I pressed Joel to find us a new home. He couldn't understand my urgency and while he tried to be supportive and please me, I could see he was not going to act. So, I located a realtor myself, and she found a house in Malibu overlooking the Pacific with expansive ocean views. Even though the new house stretched our resources, we bought it. On New Year's Eve, we watched the world welcome the millennium on TV in our new bedroom. The millennium celebrations were fun, but when it was over, the whole affair felt anti-climactic. It was just another date and another year gone by.

Our new home was nothing if not dramatic and it turned out to be the perfect setting for house parties. Joel's political interests led to our hosting fundraisers for several congressmen and senatorial candidates and even the governor of New York. One of our events was attended by the film director Oliver Stone. Many of our guests were impressed by the twenty-gallon salt water fish tank I had installed in our living room, which turned out to be a white elephant. We had goldfish when I was young, which I took care of until Rick killed them by getting a bigger fish, who ate them. Our Malibu tank was pretty spectacular with a Lion-fish, blue and yellow striped Angelfish, and a garden of sea anemones. But a salt tank is hard to maintain and, one day, the people servicing the tank put in the wrong chemicals. The next morning, we woke up to find them all dead. After that, I didn't have the heart to start over again.

Being married to Joel, I was becoming a lot more aware of politics and enjoyed many of the events he hosted both in our home and at other venues like the Arizona Biltmore and the Beverly Hills Hotel. But I was, and would always feel, a kind of visitor to this world and it didn't fill the vacancy inside me or help to answer Henry's question. My main attention was still on my son who was graduating Calvary Christian in the spring. I needed to find him another school and finally decided on Saint Monica High, which was a Catholic school. Every day, I drove him to his classes and every day, as we approached our destination, he would gag and spit up. It was a return of the anxieties he had developed at the Brentwood charter school. I tried to comfort him and felt a deep sadness witnessing his distress. It brought back memories of my childhood when I would set out from a home where Henry was usually missing and my mother was hung over or drunk, and head for school where I was often at sea. I was sure Michael's present insecurity had something to do with the fact that it was a new school and felt certain it would pass. It did as he earned excellent grades and reports from his teachers and his confidence began to build. But the discomfort he was in was still painful.

I realized my own responsibility for these trials. Like all my siblings, I was a tense person, as though always bracing for an attack. I sensed that my own anxieties must be playing a role in Michael's. Whenever there were uncertainties on the horizon with consequences that might be negative, my mind would immediately run to worst-case scenarios even though, most of the time, the fears proved unfounded. These intimations of impending disaster were not that different from Michael's anxiety about performing well at school, despite the fact that he was a good student.

In contrast to the way my mother and I were becoming closer, I felt more distant from the rest of my family, and that pained me. In particular, I was concerned about my younger sister Janie, whom I had been closest to among my siblings, and who was living in a kind of exile in Kentucky. So, I planned a trip to see her.

Janie had married an attorney named Alan who was a troubled individual with alcohol problems. The reason they were in Kentucky was that, some years earlier, Alan was fired after he was caught drunk on the job and a female subordinate, with whom he'd had an affair, accused him of sexual harassment. He had also embezzled company funds because neither he nor Janie could live within their means. To get a fresh start, he had secured a new position in a Kentucky backwater and set about persuading Janie to follow him. I urged her not to go. He was physically abusive to her, had women on the side, and even left the house for a month when he was fired until she threatened to change the locks and keep him out for good. Part of the reason I urged her not to go with him was that I was concerned about the impact the move would have on their son. But she didn't listen to me and went anyway.

I missed her and worried about her which was why I decided to make the trip to see her. I took Michael and my mother with me and Leslie and her husband came down to join us. Before we got there, I was hoping that Janie and her husband had learned from the debacle and made changes to some of the behaviors responsible—the excessive alcohol, the womanizing, and the profligate spending. But when we arrived, I saw that they were doubling down on the very indulgences that had caused their woes. Despite the drastic reduction in their income, they had bought a five-bedroom house and furnished it with complete bedroom sets, bought on credit like everything else. They built a huge swimming pool with an artificial waterfall, bought his and hers sports cars, and a pontoon boat. I felt that my sister was attempting to bury her woes by spending money she no longer had on a house she couldn't afford.

She and her husband were also partying a lot. To introduce us to their friends, they invited over what seemed like the whole neighborhood to splash in their hotel-size pool. It seemed like everyone was soon drunk. The whole scene was pretty raucous and one woman took her clothes off, even though there were children present. I looked over at my mother and saw that she was growing angrier by the minute. After our arrival, when she had taken in the sports cars and the bedroom sets, she said to me, "This spending is ridiculous." As the pool party got into full swing, she added, "My daughter is an alcoholic and has to stop."

She wasted no time in finding an opportunity to confront Janie and have it out with her. "You're an alcoholic," she shouted at her. "You drink way too much. All your friends are out of control. Your spending is out of control. You are out of control."

Janie was flushed with anger and answered her in kind. "You don't know my friends, and you don't know what the hell you're talking about." And then a predictably wounding blow, "Who are *you* to talk, anyway?" The next day, when we went to see the local Amish and view their wares, my mom and Janie weren't speaking to each other.

A few years after this, Janie came to visit us in California and announced that she and Alan were moving to Louisville where her son was set on going to college. She and Alan did a short sale on their house, stiffing the bank and other creditors, and never looked back. The move hadn't improved her domestic scene. When we were alone, she explained in a moment of unusual candor, "My husband is always wasted. I can't be alone with him without my son."

But this confession was extraordinary and not repeated. Over time, her denials, like Leslie's, became an alternate reality she inhabited and then guarded with a ferocity that no one could challenge. She was also very much like Leslie when it came to putting her own interests before others. When Alan's sister pressed Janie to repay a thousand-dollar loan she had asked for, Janie beat her so badly, the victim's screams were so loud, that neighbors called the police. It was the third time that police had to be called to her house over her domestic violence. Janie had the family anger inside her in spades.

Once Alan and Janie were settled in Louisville, I took another trip to see them, this time with Michael and one of my nieces. Their Louisville house was a new construction as big as the one they had left behind. They furnished the new home in style too, adding an expensive grand piano that no one could play. When we landed in Louisville, Alan picked us up at the airport. I asked him why Janie hadn't come. "Oh, she's busy stuffing her fat ass," he said, displaying a hostility that was jarring to the three of us. Then he pointed to a row of houses we were passing and casually said, "Hey kids, this is where we lawyers have our mistresses," causing me to wonder what was going on.

It didn't take me long to find out. Janie was cooking when we arrived and my heart dropped when I saw her. She had gained a hundred pounds and so distorted her body that it was painful for me to look at her. She had always had a wonderful shape, long legs, full breasts and a flat tummy. She probably had the best shape out of all of us sisters. Now, at 220 pounds on a 5'7" frame, she was almost unrecognizable. The bickering between them was constant and ugly and the sexual tension high. As Alan settled into his favorite chair, he barked, "Get your fat ass up and get me my wine." Janie told him to shut the hell up, but she went and got his drink anyway.

It was a strange reception for a sister and two teenage cousins, not to mention how her own son might be taking it. I could see the kids were really uncomfortable and felt I had to get them out of there, so I said, "Let's go to the mall." Janie's son drove us. On the way, I asked him if this went on all the time.

"Yeah," he answered with a downcast look, "they're always fighting." It upset me to see him like this. He had been a happy kid in California, but now a cloud of depression seemed to envelope him. To change the mood, I said, "Let's get a gag gift to help their relationship." We went to the Barnes & Noble in the mall and I bought a copy of *The Joy of Sex* to bring back as a present. I thought it might lighten the tone and cheer my sister up. Maybe it would even show the two of them how insensitive they were being to their guests. But when I gave the book to Janie, instead of laughing she said, "*Eew*," and threw it on the floor. Alan picked it up. Seeing what it was, he laughed at the gag.

"Listen, Janie," I said in an effort to bring her around, "You need to lighten up and start having fun." But she was very far from being amused.

The next evening, we all went to the mall and when we got there, Alan checked into the nearest bar. Janie wanted the kids and me to follow after him, but I was not about to do that. I said to her, "Janie, this is not happening. These kids are minors and I'm not going to take my son and my niece into a bar. Moreover, I'm not going to put them in a car that Alan is driving." It was freezing outside, so we stood in the bar entrance, waiting until Alan had his drinks. Janie then fought with him to get the keys and drove us back home.

When we got there, I hugged her and told her how great her cooking was and tried to smooth over the evening's events. We reminisced about our childhoods, gossiped about the family, and laughed together. Little did I suspect that, under the surface, she would nurse a grudge about the gag gift I had bought her for thirteen years until her anger burst to the surface and came between us for a final time.

A Death in the Family

MY LIFE BEGAN TO move in a new direction when Joel enlisted me as a photographer for the public events he put on. I had bought a camera and discovered that I had a talent for composition. At one of his events, I met Vincent Bugliosi, who prosecuted Charles Manson for the Sharon Tate murders. I told him I admired what he had done and asked to photograph him. Weeks later, he called to ask me if I would do a portrait of him to appear on the flap of a book he had just finished. He invited me to his home to do the portrait and began talking about Manson and how he thought he was a coward. Manson had used drugs to manipulate his women into committing heinous acts. But off drugs, in prison, he had thrown them all under the bus. Bugliosi thought, off drugs, Manson was a nobody. When Bugliosi's book was published, he called to tell me that my photo was his favorite portrait of himself, and asked me to have it enlarged so that he could hang it over his fireplace.

Although I was logging new accomplishments, the old restlessness had not entirely gone away. I began obsessing about the floor plan of the Malibu house, which was too spacious and un-cozy and felt un-home-like to me. The front door opened onto a room that was so big it occupied most of the one-story house, which made it ideal for house parties, but not so ideal for family living. The house was beautiful, but in some way left me feeling uncontained and insecure. Three large columns had been built to break up the space, but these gave it a cold and monumental look. I found myself longing for walls, for the comfort of ordinary rooms. I couldn't put my finger on why I felt so restless again, but before I knew it, I wanted to move. Since the house was very desirable, we were able to sell it quickly for a handsome profit and move inland to a newly built home in Agoura Hills.

The new house was a two-story Spanish stucco nestled in the coastal mountains. Even though it was a just-completed new construction, I immediately set about making changes. I put in a ten-foot-high stained glass window with grapevines to ensure privacy from the neighbors. I hired a carpenter to frame an arch in the passageway between the living room and the kitchen, ripped out the new pink and gray granite counters in the kitchen and replaced them with tiles, put in drapes to border the stained glass, and then went about land-scaping the lot it had been built on. I didn't think about it then, but later, I reflected on how I had responded after my mother's breakdown and departure when I threw myself into redecorating the house and making it something I felt was my own. It seemed to be a recurring passion with me.

Michael had graduated high school and was now living in the dorms at Loyola Marymount University where his scientific interests had begun to flower. When he told me that he had been accepted, I broke out in tears of joy. But I also felt a sadness, bordering on panic—and not for the last time—that my child had grown to manhood and was going to be out of my house and on his own. I had a very close relationship with Michael. I didn't want him ever to feel left out in the cold and by himself as I had. I was determined that he would always know and never have cause to doubt that his mother loved him, was behind him, and would always be there for him when he needed her. I tried to give him the guidance and support that I never had. But I also realized that he had guided me too. It was my love for him that had pulled me out of the darkness and confusion into which I had been brought into the world.

To comfort myself for the fact that my son was now away at college, I went out and bought a giant puppy to join our two Chihuahuas and named her Winnie. She was a Bernese Mountain Dog, a big slobbering bundle of love with large soft pink paws and a splash of white on her chest. Obviously, she could, in no way, fill the hole my son's departure created, but she did provide a ready distraction from the pain of missing him and also a comfort whenever my thoughts turned to the fact that he was no longer under my wing.

I continued to bring my mother to visit us and to stay with us for a week or more at time. On one of these occasions, she told me that Henry wasn't doing well and might have dementia. He had been in poor condition for a while, but this was the first anyone had told me about it. She said that at first Rick had insisted on keeping Henry at his house, but now was putting him in a nursing home. As Henry's biological son, Rick had always been his father's favorite among the children in our household. Henry had secured a job for him working as a manager in the company whose sales division he headed. Not long before he became ill, Henry had taken Rick—and only Rick—on a month-long pleasure trip to Ireland.

While Henry was still healthy, Rick was all over him, playing the role of the chosen son. But once Henry became ill and helpless, Rick's dark side came out and he turned with a vengeance on the father who had given him a place in the sun. It was Rick who put Henry in the nursing home and who arranged with my mother and a lawyer to make himself executor of Henry's considerable estate. During this time, one of my nieces, to whom I was especially close, went to see Henry at Rick's house. She told me he was in a wheelchair and, while she was there, he had thrown up on himself. When Rick saw it, he screamed, "You dumb sonofabitch. Look what you did."

On hearing this, despite Henry's meanness to me, my heart went out to him, especially when I realized how ill he was, although I was never told the exact nature of what was wrong with him. I had a sense that, whatever the illness was, it might be terminal, and this led to a powerful feeling that I had to see him before he was gone. Soon after the wheelchair incident, Rick committed him to the nursing home and I decided it was time for me to visit him. When I told my mother, her reaction startled me. "Absolutely not," she said. "He won't even recognize you. It's not worth your time." When I indicated that I would go anyway, she repeated, "Don't! Don't! It's not worth your time. He won't recognize you." The passion with which she said this immediately aroused my suspicions. I felt something was going on that was not right, which only intensified my determination to see for myself. When my mother realized that I was set on going, she said "I want to go with you," so I took her.

The nursing home was a grim place with bare walls and the musty smell of old age and soiled diapers. When I entered the room where Henry was, I had the wind knocked out of me. This was nothing like the man I had known. He was emaciated—so thin that the flesh had been drained from his face, causing his eyes to sink into the sockets and pushing his skull to the surface. He was not moving and looked cadaverous. His glasses were on and were almost stuck to his nose. When I lifted them to wipe his brow, I saw they had made deep dents in the bridge. Puss oozed from the cavities, revealing brownish red and yellow sores, which looked like they had been there for a long time.

The sight of him left me shaking so badly that I had to get up to leave the room. Once outside, I leaned against a wall to pull myself together. When I had calmed myself, I went back and leaned over the bed and said, "Hi, dad. Do you know who I am?"

He looked at me and said, "Melanie."

I said, "No, dad. It's Christine."

Then he said, "Of course I know who you are. You're Christine. Is Melanie coming?"

It looked like he weighed less than a hundred pounds. I noticed that there were trays of food uneaten. I asked him why he wasn't eating. "I can't eat," he rasped. "I need liquid. Can you get me a coke?" I went to the coke machine in the hall and brought him one. He gulped the coke down and asked for another.

I said to my mother "Why isn't he being fed?"

The question touched a nerve. "This doesn't concern you," she growled.

When I saw it was pointless to pursue this any further, I headed for the door and told her I was going to ask a nurse. When I found one, I said, "My dad is starving to death. He can't eat from the tray."

The nurse already knew. She said, "We had orders to take his feeding tube away." Then she explained the doctor had made the decision after Rick complained the tube was bothering Henry and instructed them to take it away. I asked the nurse if Rick ever came to see him. She said, "He came once, but that was it. I haven't seen him since." Then she said, "Rick is in control of his care. If I were you, I would try to figure out a way to get control of your dad's care and change that order." But that wasn't going to happen. Rick had seen to that.

Behind me, Henry was moaning "Hurt so much." I asked him if he would like to be sponged off. He sighed hungrily, *yes*. When I removed his shirt, his shoulders were so sunken that, as the sponge went over them, pools of water formed in the depressions created by the sagging flesh. His legs were like sticks. I felt so bad for him I could hardly hold back the tears. When I had finished, I sat by his bedside for a long time, wondering how it had all come to this. And I knew, without knowing exactly how or why, that this would produce another friction with my mother.

After I left the nursing home, Joel and I had to travel to Florida for an event Joel was hosting. While we were there, I received a call from my mother. "Henry died," she said coldly.

I started to cry, and asked her, "Mom, why was he starved to death? Why was he so neglected?"

This elicited an attack. "Why do you care?" she said. "You went off on vacation." I was taken aback by how quickly she distorted the situation to make me the guilty party.

"I am *not* on vacation," I replied; "I am here on work for my husband. This is a large event he's hosting. It's his business and I'm here to support him. Besides, the whole time Henry was starving to death, you kept saying 'Do not go to see him. He won't recognize you.' You wouldn't even tell me where he was. I practically had to threaten you to find out. What kind of a mother are you?" I hung up.

Almost overnight, without notifying anyone in the family, Rick arranged to have Henry cremated. He proceeded like someone who was disposing of a body, not burying a father. It showed his contempt for the man who had raised and been a benefactor to him. But it was also motivated by the fact that he didn't want to spend any of the money Henry had left on a funeral. My sisters and I were outraged by what Rick had done to our father, but we had no inkling of what he was about to do to us. Many years before, Henry had come to my house and said casually, "What would you think if I left you children sixty thousand dollars each in my will?" I hugged him and said, "Thank you. That was a very nice thing for you to tell me." But Rick was now the executor of Henry's estate and he used his authority to disinherit us.

The money earmarked for us that Rick took for himself was only a small part of what Henry had left, which included all the houses he had bought for his girlfriends. It ran into the millions. Rick took it all for himself, except my mother's house, which he allowed her to live in. But to show her his power and also his contempt, Rick cut off her electricity and water. She called me, crying. "My electricity and water have been cut off. Rick is supposed to manage this."

I called Tommy, who seemed familiar with Rick's plans and said, "Of course he's not going to live up to his agreement." I called Rick and confronted him with what he had done, how he had stolen the inheritances of his sisters, and now was turning the screws on his mother. He just laughed. Eventually Tommy was able to put a check on Rick's vindictiveness, telling him the electricity and water were a small price to pay to keep his mother from causing any legal trouble.

After my phone call to Rick, I went over to my mother's house and took her to ours where she stayed for weeks. While she was with us, she called Janie, who hung up on her. Leslie wasn't talking to her at all. The two of them were probably angry about the disinheritance and suspicious of Gigi's role in it. But neither of them told me why. The morning after Gigi arrived, I noticed she was walking around the house with Henry's gloves on. I confronted her. "Why are you walking around with his gloves? You know you didn't like him. All I've been hearing from you since he died was what a sonofabitch he was." When she didn't answer, I decided to ask her the questions that had been on my mind since she called me about Rick turning off the water. "What is all this, really? Just tell me the truth. What do you have going on with Rick? What did you do that you've caused your daughters to not want to talk to you?"

My words seemed to strike her like blows. She started crying hard and said, "Rick had me do a deal with him. He told me if I kept you girls away so that he could get the lawyer to control everything, he would let me live in the house until I died. He told me that he would give me a monthly allowance and would keep on the water and the electricity. He said I could use the allowance to take the girls to lunch. He said he would give the girls the house when I died." But she knew now that Rick never meant to keep his promises. The house was not going to the sisters but to Tommy, who, it turned out, was his partner in crime.

I kept this secret from Joel for a while, but soon felt I had to tell him, something I normally would never do because of the family rules. What had happened was far too upsetting to me and Joel was someone I had found I could rely on and was always ready with good advice. I needed his comfort and counsel. In retrospect, I should have kept the secret to myself. One day not that long afterwards, Joel heard my mother yelling at me in the house. We were arguing about the deal she had made with Rick. Her yelling angered him because he knew how much I wanted to please her, and that she had so alienated all her children that I was the only one who was willing to take her in and take care of her. Yet, here she was attacking me, in my house.

The revelation that she had betrayed me with Rick pushed Joel over the edge. At this point in our life together, no matter how many times I had tried to explain it to him, he still didn't understand how my family and its secrets worked. He had no inkling of the mine fields he was about to blow up. My mother adored him and wanted him to think the best of her. Now, he was accusing her of betraying her daughters by allowing Rick to disinherit them. It was especially callous of her, he said raising his voice, to betray the one daughter who looked after her when the others wouldn't even talk to her. Confronting my mother on my behalf, Joel thought he was defending me. But what he was really doing was stripping the mask from my mother's deceptions, and leaving her naked without her protections. He had taken away her victim role and made her the culprit. He had disregarded the good things she had done for me and how much she respected him. The effect was devastating; it turned her against me for good.

After Joel's outburst, when my mother and I were alone, she lit into me, unloading a stream of invectives accusing me of being the betrayer for exposing a family secret. She piled on curses, working herself into a frenzy until finally she screamed, *You're dead to me.* A black pit formed in my stomach as I realized something irrevocable had taken place. This maternal curse lasted through the next four months, which proved to be the final ones of her life, estranging us forever.

The deal to disinherit us that she had made with Rick was successful. None of us dared challenge Rick's legal conniving because, throughout our lives, we had witnessed his violent temper and behavior, and were afraid of the consequences of going against him. In a famous incident that took place when he was only eleven, Rick was given a stereo for Christmas. Even though it was the day before Christmas Eve, he wanted to unwrap the stereo and play it. He called our parents, who were out at a party to ask permission. When they heard his request, they told him no, he would have to wait until Christmas Day to open it. As soon as he hung up the phone, Rick picked up the stereo and smashed it on a table over and over until it broke into little pieces. Janie and I, who were eight and nine at the time, looked on in terror. Such displays of anger and violence grew as Rick got older and began drinking, even leading to an occasion where he physically attacked a policeman and was arrested until Henry got him released.

I was especially scared of Rick because of a traumatic event that had taken place the year before Joel and I met. It occurred on a day when I had let him pick up my son after school and bring him to his house to play with his own son, who was Michael's best friend. I had never seen Rick lose his temper with his children and he had also married a good woman. Consequently, I was comfortable with the arrangement. On this day, I stopped at their house to get Michael on my way home from work. When I arrived, they were all in the pool area. As I approached, I saw the kids disappear through the sliding doors to go into the house to play. Rick was sitting poolside, drinking a beer.

"You look tired," he said as I came up. "I am," I replied. "I've been in these high heels all day and my feet are aching." Then he asked, "Have you ever learned to swim?" I looked at him incredulously and said, "Rick, you know I don't know how to swim."

As soon as the words left my mouth, he stood up, all six feet, two hundred pounds of him, walked over to me, grabbed my arm, and began dragging me over to the pool, while I shouted "Stop! Stop!" When we reached the pool edge, he threw me into the deep end, where I sank below the water line and began to panic. I flailed my arms, and kicked off my shoes, and tried to crawl through the water to the surface. Finally, I was able to reach it gasping for air. As I did so, I caught sight of Rick's back as he hurried to enter the house through the sliding doors.

Once inside he locked the doors behind him and pulled the blinds, so the kids couldn't see what was happening. I pulled myself out of the pool, made my way to the sliding doors, and pounded on the glass until my son came and opened them. Barefoot and sopping wet, I grabbed his arm and headed for the front door, passing Rick, who was standing with his beer in the kitchen. "You motherfucker," I shouted at him. "You psychopath. You tried to kill me." My words made no impression. He wouldn't look at me and said nothing.

When I got home, I told my mother what had happened. She called Henry, and put me on the phone. Henry's voice was perfectly calm on the other end of the line, "Your brother called me and said you fell into the pool and were mad. Don't try to make something out of nothing."

I was beside myself. "It's not nothing! Rick is lying. He tried to kill me!" I made an effort to tell him what actually happened, but he didn't want to hear it. He just dismissed everything I said. My mother, standing behind me, was silent. She was not going to confront either of them. Afterwards, I tried to think of anything I might have done in the past to antagonize Rick and provoke such malice. But there was nothing. I always knew my brother had violence in him, but I had never thought of him before as a killer.

Therapy

I WAS ALONE AGAIN in the family, but at the same time, I was finding a new direction in my life which made the separation less painful and was absorbing most of my days and attention. When you find a direction, it can have the effect of changing everything, beginning with your sense of yourself. For me, this new direction involved horses. I didn't much think about it at first, but there was a family root to this interest going back to my mother's love for her lost Rosie and my Aunt Betty's life as a blue-ribbon jumper. As I got to know these noble creatures and then became involved in rescuing them, I realized the connection was much deeper. Horse rescue spoke to the sense I had of myself as a child, who could not count on parents to protect her and as a result, always felt vulnerable in a hostile world and in need of someone to come and look after her.

My interest in horse rescue had begun in our house in Agoura. The corral across the way was home to a beautiful satin black stallion with a white blaze on his forehead and the softest brown eyes you could imagine. Eventually, I learned his name was Domino. His companion was a Shelton pony named Sweetie who had matted chestnut hair so long it hung like moss from his flanks. Sweetie was so old he barely moved. Every day, I would bring them carrots, striking up a relationship which I didn't realize at the time was going to take me on paths I could not have foreseen.

The corral Domino and Sweetie were kept in was on a hillside, which is not a good footing for horses. One day, I went across the street to give them their carrots and instead of running towards me when I called out to him, Domino just stood at a distance without moving. When I called to him again, he started to move forward and I realized there was something terribly wrong. He was in great pain and was limping. I went over to the neighbor who owned him and told her what I had seen. She said she was aware of the problem and assured me a vet would be coming out to see him.

Days went by and the vet didn't come while Domino's condition grew worse. On the fourth day, he was lying on the ground and could barely raise his head. His body was tense and he had dropped so much weight that it was hard to recognize him. He was in agony from his head to his hooves, shaking and shivering. My own heart was pounding. I stepped through the pipes of the corral and climbed the hill to where he was lying to try to comfort him. He was suffering from a condition called laminitis, which is an inflammation of the lamina that connect the hoof to the bone. If not treated in time, the hoof separates from the bone and the horse has to be put down. At the time, I didn't know what laminitis was, but when I looked into Domino's eyes and saw his terror, it scared me too.

There was no shade on the hillside and the sun beat mercilessly on the suffering horse. I went back to my house and filled a bucket with water to give him a drink and cool him down. Then I went to the neighbor and knocked on her door. When she opened it, I said, "I've just looked at Domino. He's in terrible shape and so much pain. I can't bear to see him suffering like this. You said the vet was coming. Where is the vet?" The woman glared at me and said, "It takes two weeks for the vet to come," which I knew was not true. "What do you want from me?" she said urgently. "I want you to get this horse some help," I answered. "He doesn't deserve this."

The following morning, I looked out my front window and saw Domino down on the ground, shaking, barely able to lift his head. I climbed into the corral and went over to him. Even though it was early, the temperature was already in the nineties. Domino looked thinner than ever. His head had shrunk and when I touched his face, it felt like leather. I said to myself, *Domino is dying and nobody cares.* My heart was breaking. I went back to the house to get my camera, then climbed through the pipe fence again and began taking pictures. I was going to log his suffering and send the pictures to the authorities or whoever would listen. I wanted to find out what a horse's rights were. I needed to learn what one could do for a horse when his owners were so callous and cruel. As I was photographing Domino, I began crying so hard it soaked my lens.

Just then, the owner came out and said, "What the hell are you doing?"

Her tone gave me a start. I said, "I'm giving Domino a voice. I'm going to tell Domino's story."

She said, "I told you the vet is on the way."

"I don't believe you," I said.

She immediately switched to the defensive. "I have bills to pay," she said. "I don't have the means."

My tears turned to rage and I screamed at her, "What are you saying? That because you have bills, you're just going to let him die? This horse needs a vet and he needs one now. If you don't make the call, I will."

She yelled back, "The vet is coming today, so don't get involved."

That pacified me for the moment, but I didn't trust her. "If I don't see a vet here today," I warned, "I *will* get involved. I don't care what you think."

For the next few hours, I kept a vigilant watch from my front window to see if anyone came. Eventually, a woman appeared wearing a vet's smock. She bent over Domino and ran an IV into his neck. While she was doing this, I looked towards Sweetie, Domino's shaggy companion. Sweetie was standing at the far side of the turnout looking distressed. The vet and the woman got Domino up. He was so thin and weak. They walked him up the hill towards the gate to take him away. But before he reached it, he collapsed. The vet then reached into her pocket for a syringe and put him down.

They wrapped his massive frame in a sheet and pulled him up the hill, and put him in a truck and hauled him away. Little Sweetie started calling out and circling the spot where Domino had lain. Her screams went on for a long time. Then a man came down the hillside, tied a rope around her neck and led her up the hill. After that, I never saw her again.

It was then that I decided I was going to get involved in horse rescue and dedicate myself to doing something about the abuse and neglect I had just witnessed. Domino's painful, needless death had put a fire in me. I wanted to understand what rights horses had, how to help horses in need, and how to raise people's awareness about them. I wanted to open their eyes to the miraculous gift of these beautiful creatures, how they depend on us for their well-being, and how we owe them our compassion in return.

My newly found cause was a salve to my restlessness. Eventually, I came to realize that, behind this new mission, was a desire to have what would always be denied me: To somehow go backwards in time and put the Humpty Dumpty of my family together again. The best thing for suppressing the pain, I discovered, was to go outside myself and help others.

There were additional factors behind my feelings for horses and my desire to help them. While equines are physically powerful, the appearance is deceptive. Behind those big brown eyes like Domino's there is a soul that is quite frightened and helpless. Horses are prey animals and their first and almost only defense is flight. A twelve-hundred-pound stallion can be spooked by a sound as innocent as an aerosol fly spray and leap across a stall to avoid it. Once domesticated, equines are like children, wholly dependent on the kindness and concern of their human caretakers which cannot always be counted on, as I had just seen for myself. I knew from my childhood the feelings of desperation and fear that irresponsible guardians could inspire. It was no accident that helping these gentle and vulnerable creatures should become a passion for me.

At the time, I couldn't have fully articulated these thoughts. I just felt a kinship with these creatures, a love that made me want to help. I also realized that I was blessed with an emotional intuition that allowed me to be patient until I was able to understand what they wanted and how they looked at the world around them. With the help of some friends and a local veterinarian, I familiarized myself with the problem of abused and neglected horses and created a tax-exempt organization to help them. I raised money to buy the hay and medicines and veterinary services they needed. Soon, I was known around the horse barns and ranches and also to the local animal control officers, who would call me when a situation arose that required my help.

In one case, we were called to assist in what turned out to be one of the largest cases of horse neglect in California. Over a hundred horses were found on a ranch that were near death from starvation and neglect. Because of my interest in photography, I put together a film crew and had them record the rescue and rehabilitation efforts. We put the film on the Internet to raise money for the local Humane Society which handled the bulk of the rescue effort.

One of my most rewarding experiences was the rescue of a beautiful bay thoroughbred named Covergirl Cool from a "kill pen" that had already claimed the life of her young foal. A kill pen is the terminal point for retired race horses, like Covergirl, who have become too old to earn more prize money for their owners. A young woman working in the kill pen had heard about our organization and called to see if I could help Covergirl. She said, "This horse is too young and beautiful to end her life this way." I said I would.

When I first saw Covergirl, my heart stopped for a moment at the thought that someone would want to destroy her. She was as beautiful as the woman had said, and one of the sweetest horses I ever met. We bonded almost instantly and I thought to myself: This horse would make a wonderful poster girl for horse rescue. I decided to put on a show and stage a "coming out" for my new charge with the announcement of her adoption serving as its climax. With the help of friends, I persuaded the Santa Barbara Polo & Racquet Club to let us be the half-time show at the 100th Anniversary of the Bombardier Pacific Coast Open Polo Championships. With help from two friends in the advertising business, we were able to make a television spot to promote horse rescue and air it twelve-hundred times on stations from Los Angeles to the Santa Ynez Valley, reaching hundreds of thousands of people in the process.

The polo championships were attended by three thousand people. At half-time we assembled a cast of film personalities and horse lovers that included Bo Derek and Robert Davi to carry our message. Davi read a letter from

Robert Duvall, who was making a film at the time, that said, "From my uncle's ranch in Montana, to the set of *Lonesome Dove*, my fondest memories have always included horses. They are a part of the very fabric of our country. Thank you for being here to help in the effort to rescue and save this beautiful and noble animal."

As the highlight of our show, we brought out Covergirl adorned with a horseshoe wreath of roses and a banner that said, "I was saved." As she passed by the crowd, Davi said over the microphone, "Let's give her a standing ovation. This horse was left for dying and look at her now. This is what Christine and her organization have done." Then we held an adoption ceremony to provide Covergirl with a "forever home," which is the ultimate goal of horse rescue. Her new parents were the television personality Alan Thicke and his wife Tanya. Before the event, I had shown Covergirl to Tanya who immediately wanted to adopt her. Alan was working and could not attend, but Tanya was there to say some heart-felt words about our cause.

I soon learned that Tanya had not informed Alan he was adopting Covergirl. When I interviewed him for the local paper after the event he said, "When my wife and son confronted me with those big doe-y eyes and droopy faces and said, 'We have something to tell you,' I thought, 'Uh-oh, the cat died.'" When they explained who Covergirl was, he thought to himself, "Oh, great. Another horse." He already had twelve.

In fact, Alan had a big heart for horse rescue. He had already adopted four of his horses from friends who didn't have the time or inclination to take care of them. Of Cover-girl, he said, "It was very touching to save a perfectly grand horse destined for oblivion."

My efforts on behalf of abused and neglected horses connected to my most primal feelings. All through my childhood, I had longings for someone to come and pick me up, and take me to a place where I would be free from the anxiety and fear and loneliness that were a second nature to me. Now, I was doing the same for them.

Because of my rescue efforts, people would often call to ask me to be with them when their animals had to be put down. It was how I came to know a donkey named Apple Jack whose story summed up what my rescue work meant to me. When I got the call for Jack, he was in his thirties and was coming to the end of his natural life. His owner was a lady named Pat who had rescued him many years before when he was abandoned and left on his own. I got the call late at night and when I pulled up onto Pat's property, the sky was full of stars and I could see the donkey on the ground and Pat sitting beside him. I went to sit with them and saw that she had been crying. Then, after a moment of silence, without me prompting her, she began to tell me her story.

When she first encountered Jack, he was very thin and neglected. She told me she could see in his eyes that he badly wanted to be loved. She said, "Christine, look at his eyes. His eyes are the most sweet, loving eyes I have ever seen." I looked over at the donkey. He was in a poor state, breathing heavily and obviously in the last moments he would spend with us. But his eyes were still soft. He was scared and it was obvious that he wanted Pat to be there by him. She continued with her story. When she rescued Jack, her first thought was "Oh my God. What have I gotten myself into? How am I going to care for a donkey?" Pat had recently been through a divorce and soon after was diagnosed with breast cancer. But she kept the donkey, and the longer he was with her, the more she grew to love him.

After her breast cancer diagnosis, Pat went into a deep depression and was tempted to give up. But what kept her going was she knew she had to take care of Apple Jack. The bond that grew between them began to brighten her days. When she became very ill from the chemotherapy treatments, she would go out to the barn to sit next to Apple Jack; the closeness she felt to him and the need they had for each other became a comfort to her. Then another day came and she lost her job and, with it, her income. Now she needed money for both of them and was at a loss as to what to do. A neighbor suggested that she take Apple Jack around the neighborhood and give rides to the local children to make money. And that's what she did. It began with a couple of kids, but then there were several dozen and she and Jack were able to earn enough money to get by on. Pat turned to me as she told me this and said: "All Apple Jack ever asked for in return was hay and hugs and kisses."

When the vet arrived, Pat knew it was time to say goodbye. I moved back to give them some privacy and watched her kiss Jack's face, and rub his back in the spot where he liked it. He lifted his head at one point to reach out to her and give her a kiss in return. Then the vet administered the final injection and Apple Jack was released from his old, sick body and was able to move on.

It was such a blessing for me to see the love between Apple Jack and Pat and to share in their goodbyes. When it was all over, Pat said, "You know, Christine, I did rescue Apple Jack, but he saved my life. He truly rescued me."

And that was the way I had come to feel about my own work with horses. What I gave to them, came back to me, and became a lifeline that lifted my spirits and provided me with a new and stronger sense of who I was.

Gigi's Final Days

GIGI HAD TERRIFIC GENES from her mother who had lived to be ninety-eight. But even though she had given up alcohol, drugs, and cigarettes, the years of hard living had taken an alarming toll. She suffered from diabetes and was on insulin and as she approached seventy, her kidneys began to fail. Even though she had stopped drinking twenty years before, her liver was in poor shape from the alcohol abuse and she had Hepatitis C from the drug needles. Her doctors had warned us for years that she had only months to live, but she had fooled them so many times they began referring to her longevity as a miracle. Then, one evening, there was a call from one of my nieces telling me that she had passed out and couldn't be wakened. My brother, Tommy, had called an ambulance to the house to take her to the hospital.

When I heard this, I rushed to where they had taken her and were prepping her for an emergency surgery to insert dialysis tubes into her neck. She had revived in time to be scared and was crying when I arrived. I tried to calm her and told her she was going to be all right, but I could see the terror in her eyes and it would not go away. After the surgery and once they had stabilized her, they transferred her to a nursing home where she could receive regular dialysis treatments. She had lost a lot of weight, her skin was parched, and her body smelled like chemicals. When I suggested that we turn on the TV that was hung from the ceiling over her bed, she said she could only see silhouettes. I felt so bad for her and wanted nothing more than for us to be close again. But she wouldn't let go of her grievance and didn't miss an opportunity to let me know how disappointed in me she was because of the secret I had shared with my husband.

All my siblings were now middle-aged. In the unfolding of their lives I was able to see the marks of the family in which we grew up—the roiling grievances, twisted silences, and abiding miseries that accompanied them. These marks were visible in the choices they made and the life partners they selected. The whole tortured story was almost biblical in nature: the sins of the fathers visited on the children. In their lives, I witnessed the futures I had been fortunate to escape.

Like my sisters, my brother Tommy wrestled with demons and made choices that set him off course. He had a violent temper and seemed attracted to women who wanted to hurt him. After his unsuccessful attempt to derail a train when he was fifteen, he resolved to turn his life around. He went to college to study architecture and fulfill a childhood ambition. But when he was nineteen, he got a fifteen-year-old pregnant and left our house to marry her. When the baby was born, he had to drop out of school and give up his dream of an architectural career. Their marriage was troubled from the start. One evening after a fight, his wife appeared made up and decked out and told him she was going out with one of his best friends. Tommy had broken his foot and was on crutches at the time. When he refused to give her the car keys, she grabbed one of the crutches and split his head open. Shortly after that, she left him, taking their daughter with her and turning so completely against him that he had to attend her wedding as an uninvited guest whom no one in the family spoke to.

Tommy then took up with an attractive Hispanic woman named Maria who was separated from her wealthy husband. Unknown to Tommy, Maria was still seeing her husband, who became suspicious and finally found out about them. Tommy worked out regularly in a local gym and with Maria's help, the husband found out the time Tommy left the gym, when he would be physically drained. When Tommy returned to his house from a two-hour workout, the husband and a friend were waiting there to jump him. Tommy did not go down easily but fought back ferociously, wrecking the inside of his house in the process. Finally, they wrestled Tommy to the ground, pulled out a knife and cut off his ear.

A neighbor called and told us what happened. When we reached the house, the ambulance was already there, lights flashing. My brother was in the front yard, holding his head and looking for his ear. He kept saying, "My ear. I gotta find my ear." There was blood running down his neck. I felt so sorry for him. It was so sad.

Because the parents of the husband were wealthy and could afford good lawyers, he got less than a year for the assault. Tommy never found his ear and had to have painful skin grafts from his thigh to create a new one, which was little more than a flap to protect the hole. I was twelve at the time and remember visiting him with my mother and sisters in the hospital. My mother was very calm when terrible things happened and we all felt bonded as a family by the calamity. One by one, we took turns to give Tommy a kiss and tell him that we loved him. While we were there, Maria came by to apologize. My mother confronted her and told her, coldly, "It's nice of you to apologize, but you need to leave."

When Tommy's temper was under control, he was a capable and intelligent person. Over the years, he rose through the ranks in the company where he worked, until he became a factory manager and eventually supervised eight hundred employees. After his divorce, he married Earlene, a Mexican immigrant whom he met in a bar. He adopted her daughter and took in eight members of her family who were in America illegally, putting them up for years in his one-bedroom guest house. Earlene bore him three more lovely girls. Tommy was an overly-strict and controlling father, which was probably a reaction to his own upbringing. But the rules he laid down and enforced reflected his care and protectiveness, and the results were evident in his daughters' productive lives.

Earlene, on the other hand, turned out to be somewhat crazy, and very hostile. A religious Catholic, she repaid his support by spending tens of thousands of his hard-earned dollars on exorcisms in far-away places like Texas, while making his home life a living hell. At one point when the girls were in their teens, Earlene disappeared with the four of them and a lover in tow. It was only after several weeks that a phone call from one of Tommy's daughters revealed they were in Mexico, but not where. This left him in the dark as to how he could locate them or whether Earlene intended to bring them back. He was about to go to Mexico to find them when Earlene relented and returned with them. On their return, Earlene's hate for him reached new levels. She drained his bank account to underwrite a series of failed business schemes, kept her lover, and constantly let Tommy know she wished him dead. Finally, he gave up trying to appease her. They divorced and Tommy, who had been financially extorted and drained, turned his energy to colluding in Rick's scheme to disinherit his sisters after Henry's death.

Unlike Tommy, Rick had married a decent woman who raised his two children well and set them on their way. His son became a sheriff and fathered three bright boys. His daughter managed an apartment complex until her father launched a fraudulent suit against the firm that employed her, claiming that he had suffered a fall on the property because of their negligence. The firm retaliated by firing his daughter, who then devoted herself to raising her two children. Eventually, she and her brother stopped speaking to Rick because of his lies and abuses. Their mother divorced him for the same reason.

On his own, Rick turned to disposing of Henry's estate. He quit his job and proceeded to squander the stolen inheritance on prostitutes, drugs, and drug-infused purchases, including thirteen motorcycles which he bought for no particular reason. When he ran through the family inheritance, he sold the motorcycles and the houses, including his own, then drained the profits until he became penniless and homeless. Around this time, I received a call from Rick's ex-wife, who now had a new husband. She said, "Christine, I need to talk to you. Your brother Rick is homeless and living on the streets. I know you and your sisters are mad at him because he stole your inheritance, but he's threatening to kill himself and he needs someone to step in." I reminded her that she had a new husband to look after and advised her not to be dealing with Rick, who was a liar and a manipulator and needed professional help. There was nothing either of us could do to help him.

While my siblings' lives seemed to be headed steadily downhill, my own life was going in the opposite direction, filling up with rewards for the efforts I had put in. Michael was now in a master's program at UCLA and spent much of his time in its laboratories as a research scientist, pursuing remedies for AIDs. It was tremendously gratifying to see the kind of man he had become and was the source of much satisfaction for me in the choices I had made to open up opportunities for him. My only frustration was that he had entered worlds of knowledge—immunology and molecular genetics—where I couldn't follow him. I didn't feel so bad about this once I learned that Joel, who had had far more formal education than I, couldn't penetrate the mysteries of his scientific career either.

One day, Michael said to me, "Oh, by the way, mom, a group of us are going down to the ocean at seven in the morning to see me baptized. Would you like to come?" Of course, I would. When I arrived at the beach, Michael was already there with his fiancé, Mary, beside him. He had on a pair of trunks, a T-shirt, and a towel slung over his shoulders. There were seven other researchers from the labs with him. Someone asked us to form a circle and hold hands. It was winter and we were all freezing. The priest asked everyone to say things about Michael and they did, calling him inspirational, kind, and super smart.

One of them, an older man, said, "Michael taught me how to be humbler and a better person. We would make coffee in the lab office and I would say to Michael, 'Can you get my coffee?' because he was the newbie and younger than the rest of us. Then one day, I was trying to solve a research problem with two other scientists who were members of our team. Michael came by and I said sarcastically, 'Hey do you think you can solve this?' because the three of us couldn't. Michael looked at the problem for a little while and solved it. I was floored. I was so embarrassed. I said 'Who is this guy?' I had never taken the trouble to find out. When I looked into his degree and his research, they far exceeded mine. I was the one who should be getting him coffee. He taught me what it was to be a good person."

I was touched by what this man said. When it came my turn, out of the corner of my eye, I saw Michael lower his head—he was still so shy. I said, "Well for starters, Michael called me late last night to tell me this was happening. When he was born, he was also a big surprise to me: we had been told he was going to be a girl. Michael has continued to surprise me ever since. And he's always made me proud." Then I turned to the man who had spoken. "One thing I always taught my son was to think of others before himself. You've warmed a mother's heart by telling me that's who my son has become." Fighting back tears, I turned to Michael. "You've made me so proud to be your mother," I said, and hugged him. Then Michael walked out to the ocean. Our teeth were chattering as he took off his shirt, and I thought, "Oh my God. My poor child is going to freeze to death." The priest dunked him three times, then he came running out and we all went to breakfast.

The one sadness I had from that day—and from many others like it—was that my mother was not there to see what her grandson had become. She had taken such good care of him while he was growing up and was so instrumental in getting him to read and so interested in his developing mind. I felt the happiness she would have had if she could have seen him now. But she had squandered this opportunity as she had so many others, and there was no way back.

Michael and Mary had been together for four years, which was the amount of time I had made Joel wait until we got married. They held off another two years before finally tying the knot in our backyard. "Backyard" really doesn't do justice to the site of their wedding, since we had landscaped the half-acre wooded area at the far end of the lawn, planted elaborate flower beds, and built a gazebo where the cere- mony took place. Michael had strung lights from the trees, which gave the event a magical quality for the two hundred people—family and friends—who came to celebrate. I was a very happy mother and mother-in-law. Michael had found a life partner who was a sweet and caring person and a professional nurse, whom I knew would be a wonderful mother when the time came.

Not long before this chapter was closing in my life, I passed a milestone in my rescue work. In 2011, the rescue organization I had created was named an official charity of the Kentucky Derby. It meant national recognition and a chance to bring our message to a larger audience than we had ever had before. Senator Fred Thompson, who was a friend of Joel's agreed to be our official spokesman for the event.

At first, I found the whole prospect overwhelming. What should I wear for the red carpet and the charity ball? How was I going to pick a bonnet, which was a required accessory for female Derby-goers? What should I say when I was interviewed on the TV shows they were lining up for me and to the international press? My heart was aflutter for weeks in anticipation. When it got too intense, I settled myself with the thought that I was doing it for the horses, and even though I had never done anything like this in my life, I was going to do it now.

There were so many people who had come for the 137th running of the Derby—over 160,000 in all—and so much food, so many booths, and so much color. When I finally did my walk on the red carpet, it was not as intimidating as I had anticipated and the ball that evening was actually a lot fun. The actress Jennifer Tilly was there, along with

Vicki Gunvalson from *Real Housewives of Orange County,* Penguins' hockey star Sidney Crosby, and many other celebrity types. I enjoyed the two days I spent at Churchill Downs, but after all the stress of an event that was so much larger and more extravagant than anything I had ever been to, I didn't have the emotional room to take in the races themselves.

Nine months after my son and his bride were married in our backyard, they headed east where he was accepted by the medical school at Colorado University. Their departure was not only a rite of passage for them, but for me as well. Michael had been so much a center of my existence from the moment the two of us became an independent family, it was wrenching to realize that this was a chapter that had closed in my life. The two of us had travelled such a long distance since the days I worried how I would manage to raise him, or make my own way in the world. My love for him and concern for his future had been my guiding star through those hard years. In a way, he was my Apple Jack. Now he was moving a thousand miles away. Though I stayed in contact with him almost daily, he was embarking on a career and family of his own, and I knew it would not be the same.

My own family was changing too. Gigi died just before Michael and Mary left for Denver. With the exceptions of Janie, who could not come, and Rick and Helen who boycotted in protest, the family gathered at her funeral. After entering the chapel, the first member I spotted was my sister, Leslie, who was standing off to the side. A beauty in her youth, she was now in her late fifties and still put a lot of effort into making herself attractive. I went over to where she was, but instead of a hello, she addressed me sharply, "Can you believe Janie is not here?"

The hostile tone was jarring yet familiar. My sisters were always looking for the faults in others. But Leslie's jibe was also unfair. I already knew Janie wasn't coming because I had called her several times to see what her plans were and then to beg her to come when she said she couldn't. The edge in her voice on the other end of the line was upsetting, but even more so the fact that she refused to tell me why she couldn't make it, leaving me to draw my own conclusions. Years later when we revisited the incident, Janie explained that her husband had suffered a mental breakdown and she was afraid to leave him alone. If she had told me this at the time, I wouldn't have kept begging her to change her mind or felt so hurt when she didn't and wouldn't give me a reason why. Concealment of any weakness or shame was Janie's first priority, even from people who loved her. Denial was her first defense in any crisis that affected her.

While Leslie and I were chatting, my sister Melanie came over, startling both of us with her appearance. Melanie, who was also in her fifties, was wearing a bright red top over a crimson mini-skirt that was so brief its hem barely reached the thigh-high black stockings completing her outfit. The effect was rakish to the point where it seemed like a calculated provocation. I had always taken a sister's pride in Melanie's voluptuous beauty, along with the flair that set it off, though sometimes I had to admit that she crossed the line of what was appropriate. Even so, I was taken aback by this outfit, and the fact that she had shown up to the funeral in a way that seemed designed to broadcast disrespect.

Because I adored her, I decided to ignore how she was dressed, and accompanied her as she went up to the coffin. As we came alongside it, the sight of our mother lying there struck Melanie with a visible force and abruptly changed her mood. It was reassuring to me to see the look of defiance vanish and be replaced by a flood of emotion for our dead mother. I was equally relieved by her request that I should stand behind her when she bent over the railing for a final heartfelt kiss, ensuring that her raised skirt would not expose too much flesh.

My sister Katie had also shown up, accompanied by a festively outfitted entourage that included her husband, her fourteen-year-old daughter, and her daughter's twenty-eight-year-old boyfriend. Katie and her daughter were sporting large Hawaiian blossoms in their hair, along with burlesque eyelashes and glitter, as though they were showing up for a party. As a teenager, Katie had been the most perfect beauty among the six of us girls and, like Melanie, a Homecoming Queen. But the meth addiction to which she had succumbed early had ruined her looks. I had not seen her in years and was shocked by her current state.

When I went over to greet Katie and her entourage, it was apparent that all four of them were high. Not far into our greetings, my sister put her face close to mine and, looking directly into my eyes, said, "You know I need money. Are there going to be checks for us today?" The question caught me off guard and when I failed to answer, she repeated it, "When do we get our checks?"

As coldly as I was able to formulate the words, I said, "Katie, our mother's funeral isn't even over," and walked away.

Just before they closed my mother's coffin, I went up to see her again. In my hands were three items she had asked for months before. They were a pen, a mug and a sweatshirt bearing the logo of the organization I had created to rescue horses. I placed the items beside her and kissed her for the last time.

When the coffin was finally closed and everyone was leaving for the gravesite, my sisters came together in a tearful huddle. Melanie said, "This is all messed up. Mom's gone," and started to cry. In that moment, I felt like we were little girls again, even though, as the youngest, I was already in my mid-forties.

Leslie felt it too and said, "Do you realize we're all orphans now?"

At these words, more tears flowed. "My God," I thought, "we are a family right now." It was as though I had forgotten once again the way the years had pushed us apart, how the silences we maintained and the secrets we kept had come between us, and turned us into strangers.

I Know Who I Am

MY MOTHER'S DEATH WAS especially hard on me because of our final fight and the wounds that she had made sure would never be healed. I felt guilty for giving up the family secret that had driven her from me, which I could not undo now. But even though the book had closed, I continued to reflect on our relationship and try to find a way back to her. In doing so, I began to re-think the conflicts with my mother and also my siblings and the way I had taken on guilt as a matter of course for whatever happened. I didn't come to a firm resolution of these dilemmas until a sequence of events led to a confrontation, which stripped the veil from all our secrets and caused a final, irreparable break, bringing our family saga to an end.

After Michael and Mary left for Colorado, I was involved in a terrible automobile accident that nearly cost me my life. I had set out to drive myself to a physical therapy session to treat a neck problem that was triggering serious migraines. The day before, I had suffered one so severe I had to check into the emergency room at our local hospital for treatment. I have no idea whether the drug they administered was still lingering in my body the next morning when I left for my session, but when my truck rounded a curve not too far from my home, I was seized by a bout of dizziness which caused me to slide off onto a soft shoulder, then pitch through a flimsy fence and plunge down a steep incline.

Suddenly, I realized I was airborne and thought: *This is it; I'm going to die.* My truck had gone off the edge of a thirty-foot agricultural drainage pipe and smashed into the steel wall on the other side, totaling the truck and knocking me out. When I woke, the wrecked truck was on its side and I was suspended in mid-air by my seat belt. The airbag had failed to open and the impact of the crash had slammed me into the door, breaking my collar bone and five ribs, and puncturing my lung. Only the steel of the cab, which remained intact, saved me.

For several minutes, I passed in and out of consciousness, screaming my husband's name and crying for help. A Hispanic man who had climbed down the slope entered the cab and cut the seat strap to free me. When the paramedics arrived, I was only half conscious as they lifted me out of the wreck and into an ambulance, which rushed me to the same emergency room I had been in the day before. After the initial examination, I was moved to the Intensive Care Unit where they kept me for over a week. Doctors kept coming in to monitor my condition and particularly my heart, which had been severely bruised. One of them told me, "You're lucky. If that contusion had filled your heart with blood, you would be dead. As it is, you can be thankful to be alive."

For a long time, it felt like I was barely alive. I was weak and my left side was a cauldron of neuropathic pain. My psychological state was shattered too. When you come that close to death, it can seem to be lurking around every corner. I didn't know if I would ever be able to raise my arm again or ride my horses. One day, shortly after I left the hospital, it all came home to me. I was in my tack room, looking at my lunge line, feeling that there was no way I was going to be able to crack it and work my horses again. A black cloud descended on me. I thought, "My body is broken, my life is changed forever."

In my damaged state, I needed help with our household and getting around since, in my condition, I couldn't drive. In these circumstances, I reached out to my sister Janie who had returned from her decade-long exile in Kentucky. During that time, her husband had suffered at least one nervous breakdown and I suspected that she had too. It was evident that something was wrong between us because she remained distant after her return and, though I made many efforts to connect with her, resisted a face-to-face meeting. A year after she arrived, I still had not seen her.

Then, one evening, I was returning from a local rodeo in my truck, when she called my cell from her house. After a hello, she said—actually whispered—that she had to go to another room, so she could speak to me "in private." When she got there and resumed the conversation, she lowered her voice to a whisper again and said, "Christine, I need you to drive out here and I need fifteen-hundred dollars. Don't come to my house, but meet me at the local Denny's restaurant." The odd request and her secretive tone made me wonder exactly what was going on. I asked her directly what the money was for, but she brushed off my question saying, "Oh, just for things. Oh, we're perfectly fine." This only prompted more suspicions. Here was a request for a considerable amount of money coming from someone who was whispering in her own house, wanted me to meet her secretly away from her house, and hasn't wanted to see me for a year. "I have to ask my husband," I said.

When I told Joel about the call and the request for money, he didn't like the sound of it, particularly the fact that she hadn't wanted to see me for so long and then asked for money. He also thought that, even in the best circumstances, she was a poor risk for a loan and it would never be repaid. After discussing it, we agreed I would say no. I called Janie to tell her. She was furious. She put her sister-in-law on the phone, and in the background, I could hear her yelling "You don't care about anyone but yourself. You treat me like shit." I shouted something back and hung up.

Her behavior shouldn't have surprised me. From the time we were little, Janie was known in our family as "the shit starter," the one who liked to provoke conflicts and cause trouble. Despite our closeness, she had enough anger towards me that it often resulted in attacks that were both verbal and physical. One time, when we were adults, she punched me in the face without warning and broke my glasses. I always suspected there was an element of jealousy behind these attacks, like the long-ago fiasco over my high school boyfriend, Ronnie. Since these bursts of hostility persisted over the years, I also thought they might be triggered by my marriage, my son's achievement, or my success with horse rescue.

After our contentious phone conversation, I did what I always did when such conflicts arose. I called her and attempted to repair the breach by acting as though nothing very significant had happened. The fact that our family regularly swept unpleasant incidents under the rug made it easy to go on with the relationship as though everything was normal and nothing had happened. I began the first call by saying, "Janie, I love you. Let's just get over this." And she answered, "Whatever. Yeah, yeah, yeah." In that way, the issue was never addressed. Over the next months, we talked several times and then she showed up with her husband at our house to attend a barbecue to which I had invited her.

Why did I persist in this pursuit of a connection since it was clear that she was harboring major anger towards me that she didn't want to talk about, let alone resolve? Obviously, I was unwilling to take a hard look at what might be causing that anger or ask myself whether, in fact, it could ever be assuaged. I already knew from the countless times such issues had come up between us, going back to when we were little girls, that she would never look at them a second time, never concede that she might have been at fault in any way. Given her attitude, I was left with a choice I couldn't make. I didn't want to risk losing her by holding my ground or walking away. I didn't want to turn my back on the good times we shared together. I loved Janie. As little girls and the youngest members of the family, we had turned to each other when the traumas of the household became too scary and the violence came too close.

One episode that has stayed with me till now was an evening when Janie and I were about six and seven. Gigi had put us in the tub together and bathed us. Then she put on our long flannel nightgowns. Mine was pink and Janie's was blue, and we had matching patterns of little flowers and ruffles. Janie had a cute pixie cut. After Gigi dried us, she brushed our hair out. I noticed then that she was tense, as she often was on a day when Henry was returning from a long absence. To keep our heads from moving, she would hold our chins while she brushed. But on this occasion, she was holding mine too tightly.

When we were ready, she ordered us to the dinner table, and said, "You're going to have crackers and chili." Then she laid down napkins for us, and said "Don't spill anything. Your father's coming home tonight." As soon as we began to eat, Janie spilled a little of her chili on the table, which set Gigi off. "Goddamn it!" she said. "I meant it. Sit up and eat right."

For a moment, her stern mood put us on our best behavior. But then she left the room and we began talking and giggling. Janie picked up her spoon, the chili dribbled down her chin again, and onto her night gown. She tried to clean it, but as she did so, our mom re-entered the room. The look on her face was fearful, as though we had burned the house down. Suddenly, in a violent gesture, she grabbed Janie by the arm and dragged her across the kitchen to where the knives were kept. Opening the drawer with her free hand she grabbed one of the knives. Then she pulled Janie's nightgown towards her and began slashing it with the blade. "Goddamn it," she screamed, "I'm going to fucking kill you kids," and kept cutting wildly at the nightgown until it lay shredded on the floor. We were terrified and couldn't move. Then she put a shirt on Janie and sat us down again, and said "Eat."

The memory of this incident has never left me, and each time it comes up, I think if my mom had missed the nightgown once, she could have stabbed her little girl. Scenes like this were a big part of why I felt so bad for Janie now. We were like the children of a war zone who had suffered in ways no one outside our family could ever understand. The internal scars that Janie bore were invisible to others, but not to me and I wanted to help her. My feelings about this were so strong that it didn't occur to me that she might not want my help, and might even resent it.

As the youngest in our family, Janie and I had been especially close. Faced with her withdrawal after her return to California, all I could think about was how I wanted that closeness again. In all the years and with all the incidents that separated us, I never gave up hoping that I could make these conflicts go away and get her to see how much I loved her. That hope was really my fear of losing the only family I had.

Consequently, after my accident and despite everything, I didn't hesitate to reach out to her for help. If she agreed to come and give me a hand with the household chores and drive me to my doctors, it would also be an opportunity to give her money and provide her with other things that she needed. It would create an opportunity for us to be sisters again. When I proposed this arrangement to her, she readily agreed and was immediately helpful and supportive. It was the warm side of Janie I loved. She would stay with us for weeks at a time, returning to her home only on the weekends. She shopped for us, cooked, did the laundry, and drove me to my medical appointments.

Most of the time, we had a lot fun. Janie loved animals and would bring her aging boxer Max, whom she loved, to play with our dogs. We talked about old times and laughed a lot. The two of us had a similar sense of humor—a sort of gallows humor, turning bad things into laughter. I tried to repay her by providing her emotional and financial support. I gave her checks, put tires on her car, got her teeth fixed, signed her up for Weight Watchers and even got her a mammogram. We dined out a lot together at restaurants I knew she couldn't afford and when Max eventually died of old age, I bought her another boxer.

At the same time, there were a couple of untoward occurrences, which should have aroused my caution and prompted second thoughts. On one occasion, only weeks after my car accident and return from the hospital, when my body was still in serious pain and my sense of security still shaky, she drove off in my truck leaving me behind in a mall parking lot. It was her idea of a prank. I had no cell phone to call anyone, and no way to get home. Feeling vulnerable and abandoned and not a little hurt, I had to wait for her return.

On another occasion, we were taking the boxers along the neighborhood streets for a walk, when we came upon a young girl walking her horse. Max, who had already bitten two people and been impounded for it, was straining at his leash, barking ferociously and attempting to charge. This could have spooked the horse and created a very dangerous situation for the girl. I tried to get Janie to pull Max over to the other side of the street, but this only provoked an argument. I was so fearful of what might happen to the girl and so appalled by Janie's lack of concern that I grabbed Max's leash and pulled him over myself. As I did so, she rammed my injured left shoulder with hers. The frayed nerves from my broken clavicle and ribs were still electric, and the blow resulted in shock waves of pain. I turned around and said, "Really, Janie? You're going to hit me? Knowing my collar bone is broken? Really?" Janie was unfazed. "It's always all about you," she replied. "It's always about you and your fucking horses. All you're worried about is your reputation."

I was taken aback by the accusation. "It was about the safety of that girl," I protested. "There are laws about giving the right of way to horses." I pointed out a sign on the very street where we were standing, warning pedestrians to watch out for the horses in our neighborhood. But it was useless to argue with her, and her tirade continued all the way home.

I didn't even mention these episodes to my husband. Acknowledging them seemed too threatening, and I couldn't trust him not to confront Janie over them or throw her out of the house. I was still grateful for her help, as well as for her company. I was still worried as to what I would do without her.

Some months into our arrangement, she asked me to lend her two thousand dollars—a larger "loan" than the one

I had previously denied her. Its purpose, she said, was to pay for a test that would allow her husband to get a job and improve their family situation. My husband thought it was as fishy as her previous loan request, but I gave her the money. I did so without a thought as to whether she was telling me the truth or not, and I did it knowing she would never pay it back. I couldn't get out of my mind that she and her family were hurting, and I was still grateful for all she had done. I did it also because there were constant reminders—and she didn't even have to bring them up—that I should feel guilty for being me. The two of us would be walking through a mall or entering a store when someone would say to her, "You have a beautiful daughter," meaning me—even though I was a year older. It was her obesity that threw them off. At moments like this, I felt a deep hurt for her and though she said nothing, I knew it roiled deep emotions inside her. But there wasn't anything I could do about it.

Then, one evening, we were driving back to the house from a shopping trip. The intimacy of our talk encouraged me to try to get closer to her by revisiting a twenty-year-old conflict. The dermatologist I worked for knew her husband, Alan, and had heard him say that he intended to divorce her. I was distressed when I heard this. I felt protective for my sister and turned to my mother for advice. She had a very sour view of Alan and his philandering and the fact that Janie put up with it, but told me to say nothing. Then, without discussing it with me, she called Janie and reported what I had said. Janie brushed the information aside and immediately went on the attack, calling me a "habitual liar" who couldn't be trusted. When my mother told me this, I began to protest, but she said, "Oh, that's just the way Janie deals with hurtful truths. She makes up lies to deny them and no one can persuade her otherwise. I know my daughter."

Over the next twenty years, Janie and I never discussed this incident, but I was still hurt to think that she had regarded what I had done as an attack on her, when I only wanted to protect her. Because we were now spending a lot of time together and felt like sisters again, I wanted to try to heal this wound, so I brought it up in the car ride back to the house. I should have known better. Although everyone in the family was aware that Alan was unfaithful to her, she did not want anyone openly acknowledging it. Because wounds like this were never addressed, they were always lurking under the surface, waiting to bleed again. The moment I mentioned the incident, I regretted doing so. Her response was so emotionally violent, it led to the worst fight of our lives and the end of our relationship.

Before I could catch my breath, she was accusing me of lying, and lying she said because I was having an affair with the dermatologist who provided the information. This made no sense as an explanation for what happened but was a new attack on me. In fact, I had never had a romantic interest in the dermatologist, had never dated him, and had never slept with him. I vehemently denied I had ever had such an affair, which only caused her to repeat the accusation—and escalate it. As "proof" that I had, she claimed she had seen me crying hysterically when the alleged affair ended and my employer rejected me. The extravagance of this lie was so great, it left me momentarily speechless. Janie knew how conservative I was in these matters, how I had rebelled against the promiscuous ways of our family. But by attempting to reason with her I had stepped inside her fantasy. Her lies were so demeaning and so extreme, I realized in horror that what she was saying—screaming, actually—had nothing to do with setting a record straight, but was a violent attack on me for reasons she could not bring to the surface.

When we returned to the house, her fury continued. Jabbing her finger at my chest, she said, "I will never forgive you that you didn't give me that money." It was a reference to the $1500 she had asked me for a year before.

"Is that what this is all about, *money*?" I replied angrily. "I've given you thousands of dollars."

She ignored me and turned to a new attack. "You brought pornography into my household," she hissed. It took me a moment to realize she was referring to the *Joy of Sex* gag gift I had given her when I visited her in Kentucky thirteen years before. It shocked me that she could have nursed such a ludicrous grudge for all those years—one that even her husband didn't believe.

"I didn't know Barnes & Noble sold pornography," I said sarcastically. But I already knew that when fictions are this big, there is no way to refute them. I was hurt to the core by Janie's lies and even more by what I realized was the hatred they reflected. "Janie," I said, hoping to stop it. "Let's just agree to disagree. Let's sleep on it. We can get over this in the morning." Then I went to bed.

In the morning, it got worse. Jabbing her finger again, her voice seething, she began the day saying, "*You* owe me an apology." Turning to my husband, who was in the room with us, she then said, "You don't know who you're married to." This assault on my marriage was another bridge too far. She brought up the Kentucky story again and accused me once more of bringing "pornography" into her household. She then piled on another charge—that I had driven drunk with her son in my car. But I didn't even have a car to drive in Kentucky; it was her son who drove *me* around in his. Moreover, I was not a hard drinker and never got drunk. It was she who wanted to take the kids into the bar with Alan and would have let him drive us home in his inebriated state. The lies were so extreme and so malicious and so obviously an effort to undermine my marriage, that I had to turn away in disgust.

Finally, I had had enough. "Please go home," I said calmly but firmly. "This needs to stop. I will not be talked to like this in my home and in front of my husband. Let's just take a break." Then I went into the bedroom and wrote her a check for five hundred dollars. I still felt she was needy and was still worried about how she would get along and for some perverse reason, felt guilty for bringing up the incident that triggered her tirades. When I handed her the check, she grabbed it like it was owed to her and left.

The next day, my sister Leslie called, and asked, "What's going on?" I told her I felt like I had just been through the Vietnam War and went over what happened. Leslie knew Janie well and had even warned me that I was "crazy" to take her into my house. "I told you she was going to attack you.

There's a side to her that's very mean and out of control." I then asked Leslie what Janie had told her about our argument. "Oh, Janie said you had a disagreement, but it was nothing and will blow over." It was a familiar refrain and might have ended the episode, except that this time, Janie's attacks had produced a seismic change in me. For the first time, I was allowing myself to see the depths of her hatred, and for the first time to recognize that the hatred was not for anything in particular that I did, but for *me*.

When a week went by and I didn't hear from her, I sent an email. In it, I confronted her with what she had done, but still concluded it by reaching out to her. The separation was proving too painful for me, making me unable to hold onto what I had seen. So, I ignored what I knew and hoped that a truthful exchange between us would close the distance. If she acknowledged even partially what she had done, I was more than ready to accept my share of the blame for setting it off, as the price for having my sister back again. But it should have been obvious that this was not going to happen. I was merely fooling myself to think that it was something I said or some misunderstanding that led to her attacks.

In her reply, Janie ignored every issue I had raised. The only thing she actually responded to was my appeal to draw back from the brink, which she rejected. Because I was irrational and a liar, she said, nothing could be fixed and there was nothing to talk about. "You get these thoughts in your head, then you believe them with nothing to stand on but cheap gossip. I realize life is too short and I'm too old to continually defend my character against twisted accusations and lies. It breaks my heart that you believe what you want to believe, and there is nothing I can say or do that's going to change your opinion."

And that was it. I hadn't actually made any "accusations." This was just her way of characterizing my attempts to defend myself from what she was saying about me. But when I denied I had slept with the dermatologist or driven her son drunk, in her view I was accusing her of being a liar. And for that, I was supposed to apologize. It was hopeless. At the end of Janie's email, she wrote, "Please STOP!!! contacting me." So, I did.

Leslie and I continued to talk to each other for a while after this, but I knew our relationship was also coming to an end. In one of our conversations, she told me that she and Janie were going to help Tommy empty our mother's house, which had been vacant since her death five years before. The house belonged to Tommy now and he was ready to sell. When Leslie told me this, I knew that Janie would turn both of them against me and would make it her business to do the same with every member of the family she could. Some were beyond her reach. Katie was lost to drugs and Helen had long ago taken herself out of our lives. My mentally challenged brother, Joey, was also out of bounds and Rick was hostile to us all and would not be recruited. So, it would basically be those three.

My one concern was that they should turn Melanie against me, whom I loved, and to whom I had recently grown quite close. It would devastate me if she were to join them. I called Melanie and told her what had happened. I was very anxious about her response and said, "Melanie, I just hope you know who I am." When she said she did, it was like a great weight lifted from me. I was reassured not only by what she said, but by her tone when she said it, which let me know she shared with me a recognition of what was the deepest problem in our family—to know and hold on to the truth of who we were in the face of the cover ups and lies about us. I was still a little nervous, but I felt confident after our exchange that, in Melanie, I had an ally who cared about me and saw things as I did.

Not long after our phone conversation, Melanie and her husband, Charlie, came in from the desert where they lived to look in on his mother who was suffering from dementia. Tommy lived in the area and they stayed with him. While they were there, Janie and Leslie visited. According to Melanie, they used the occasion to attack me for what seemed like hours, only stopping when she had had enough, and told them so. When they saw she was not going to join their war party, they warned her not to talk to me. But Melanie was not going to be intimidated and said, "She's my sister, I can't go along with that."

The next day, Charlie went to see his mother, leaving Melanie alone in Tommy's house. Around mid-morning, Tommy's dog began coughing up blood. Because she had no car to take the dog to the vet, Melanie called Janie for help. But instead of providing help, Janie called Tommy to tell him what had happened, and he soon came barreling into the house. "Don't get into my fucking business," he shouted at Melanie, "and don't call people about my fucking dog." As he said this, he grabbed Melanie by her throat and slammed her against the wall. Like me, Melanie wanted to overlook the bad in people and reach out to the good. But this violent attack showed her how dangerous that attitude could be. Tommy's assault was an awakening for her as to just how far things had gone and how irretrievable they had become.

The order of battle was now set for the war that Janie had declared. Being threatened by the same forces had the effect of strengthening the bond between Melanie and me. A space opened in which we were able, for the first time in our lives, to talk frankly about the past, the family, and ourselves. The revelations that followed changed my view of Melanie, of our parents, and finally of myself.

It began quite innocently as we compared notes about growing up. We had been separated by our age gap as children and then by physical distances after she ran away and was out of touch for long periods of time. But now, we were both in our fifties and the age gap no longer mattered. "It was such a bad childhood," I began by saying. This was an obvious but—for us—unusually truthful observation, which had an immediate effect on us both.

In response, she asked me a question that was like mine with much deeper meanings than appeared on the surface. "You believe me, don't you?" she asked in a plaintive tone of voice. Her appeal had an urgency that I understood well. Hovering over it was the cloud that Melanie had always lived under—a cloud created by her parents. To cover up their crimes they had stigmatized her as a "drug addict" and "out of control" and, of course, a "liar," which was the first line of attack against anyone who told the truth in our family about our family.

I told Melanie that, of course, I believed her, but when I was little, I didn't understand everything and didn't even now. It was an opening for her to share with me what had happened to her and to know her for who she really was for the first time. "Do you remember when I ran away?" she asked.

"I do remember," I said. "I was sad that you were gone, but our parents were saying you were a drug addict and a liar."

She said, "I just smoked pot with my friends like everybody did. I ran because I had to get away from the abuse in that house."

Then she explained to me what had happened and unlocked the darkest family secret of all. "Do you remember how I took you and Janie aside, before I ran away? The two of you were seven and six, and I wanted to warn you—to save you from Henry's abuse. I was scared that you two would become his next victims. For years, I felt guilty that I had to leave you behind. You were both so little I couldn't tell you in detail what happened. I just said I love you and you can call if you need me."

I listened in shock as she told me her story. Although I was aware of many aspects of it, I never knew the true horror of what had happened to her. She was three years old when Henry began molesting her. He would announce to the family that he wanted to spend "special time with Melanie" and take her for car rides to get candy. When they were in the car together, he would ask her to touch him, touch his penis, and he would touch her. He did it gradually, but regularly. He told her she was his special little girl. "Hey, go with me to put gas in the car," he would say. When she was with him, he would tickle her and kiss her and rub her back, and then do the touching.

There were even family sessions to normalize his behavior. I remembered these from the perspective of a three- or four-year-old. We littlest members of the family would be watching a Disney show in the living room and Henry would be lying on his recliner naked. Even as little kids, we thought this was strange, but our mother would brush our questions aside, saying "Oh, he'd be a nudist if he could be; he doesn't even think about it." She would sit next to him on the recliner playing with his penis. We were too young to understand what was going on, but I didn't want to look in their direction. Melanie, who was thirteen by then and able to understand, was disgusted.

Henry began to penetrate—to rape—Melanie when she was eleven. When I asked her what she felt, she said, "I just blanked out. It was almost like I left my body. I was also terribly confused. He made me want to feel it was all because I was so special. I felt love for him, as my father. I didn't know what to think. Then I started to feel it was wrong. I didn't like it." Finally, she rebelled. She complained to her mother, "He raped me," she said to Gigi, "I can't do this. I can't take it anymore." She begged Gigi for help. But instead of comfort and support, she got an explosion. "Shut your fucking mouth right now," Gigi said; "You're a liar."

With no support at home, Melanie turned to a school counselor, confiding in her what Henry was doing. The counselor offered to help and even to take her in, but said she would first have to go to the authorities and tell them what was going on. As soon as she was sixteen, Melanie left home and went to live with the counselor. They reported Henry to the authorities and a court trial was ordered. At the trial, Melanie told her story and the counselor testified that she would be willing to provide Melanie with a home.

Henry had hired high-priced lawyers to defend him at the proceeding. He testified that Melanie was always a disturbed child and that his alleged abuse was just his determination to provide her with special attention and affection. "It was so upsetting to me," Melanie said of Henry's testimony. "But what broke me was when our mother got up and said I was a drug addict, and a party animal and a liar. She *knew* he had been raping me, but she defended him."

The judge seemed to agree. He rebuked Gigi, who had come to court in an alcohol-infused state. "I think you're the one on drugs, and you need to be quiet," he scolded her. But his hands were tied. He told Melanie he could put her in foster care and sign a restraining order for her parents. But then she would be separated from her family. Melanie was afraid of losing contact with her sisters and brothers. After weighing her options, she decided to stay until she was eighteen, but keep clear of the predator. Only once was her plan tested. It was on a night when everyone was asleep and Henry was able to slip unnoticed into her room, naked, get underneath the blankets, and spoon her thinking she was asleep. When she felt him touch her, she coughed out loud. This was enough of a signal to let him know she was not going to submit silently, which scared him, so he left.

When Melanie turned eighteen, she left our house for good. She was a beautiful young woman and smart, but carrying a psychological weight that no one should have to bear. Despite her traumas, she set out to make a life for herself. She supported herself through college, earned a business degree, and pursued a career in management, eventually becoming head manager for the local branch of a well-known retail chain. The psychological abuse she had suffered was harder to overcome. "It took me fifteen years of therapy to deal with this," she told me, "to understand that I didn't cause this, and to stop acting out as a way of burying the hurt, which ended up hurting me. When I came to mom's funeral in my outrageous red miniskirt, it was to say to her, 'Well here I am: your party animal daughter. How do you like it?' But when I saw her lifeless in the coffin, it all went out of me. It didn't matter anymore. It was just my mother, and she was gone. The anger I had towards her was suddenly useless. When I let it go, I was able to love her again. I didn't forget what she had done—how she had betrayed me and protected the rapist—but I forgave it."

"Over the years," she explained, "I hurt myself a lot because of the rage inside me. I was constantly wanting to punish men and those who had betrayed me and check out of reality, finding self-destructive ways to do it. My husband persuaded me I needed professional help and I learned to look at what my behavior was doing to me and stop striking out against the world." After two failed marriages, she had finally found peace with Charlie, a partner who would support her. They have been married for nearly twenty years and she has been blessed with two fine children and five healthy grandchildren.

What Melanie revealed to me about her childhood was terrible, and it shook me to the core. I had known Henry was an abuser, but never the depths of his depravity. Molester of a three-year-old child, rapist of an eleven-year-old, and God knows what other sexual crimes he had committed. Every one of the "girlfriends" he had set up in homes, Marge, Leilani, Lennie—and who knows what others?—had one thing in common: small children. He was a monster. I felt unclean to have known him, let alone to have had him as a father. I started to ask myself if he might have preyed on other victims in the family. Was it Helen, the oldest, who was the first to flee? Was it Rick, who hated his father so much he starved him to death and squandered his estate? Was it Tommy, who, during their fight had yelled at Melanie, "Do you think you're the only one who was raped?" All my life, I had struggled to keep a piece of my heart open to this man who had been the only father I had. But with Melanie's revelations, I felt my heart close. He repulsed me.

My mother's betrayal was a much harder cross to bear. I was forced to ask myself: Who *is* this woman, my mother? How could she have covered for this predator and served as his accomplice? How could she have betrayed her baby and protected the man who raped her daughter? How *could* she? Through all my adult life I had wanted, in every fiber of my being, to bring the family together. I had kept the silences the family exacted as the price for its unity. When the silences were broken and the knives came out, I had examined myself to see if it was I who was at fault. And did so even now. Even while I was repelled by what I had learned about my mother, I still felt for her, even thinking that guilt over her betrayal of Melanie might have triggered the mental breakdown she suffered. Nor could I forget the kindnesses she had shown me, including her help in raising my son.

One belief I had held onto since I was very young was the importance of forgiveness. I saw how grievances became corrosive if you held onto them. Being willing to forgive was less important for the person you forgave than it was for yourself. If you were willing to let things go, as Melanie had let go of her anger at our mom, you could open your heart. You could breathe again. I took comfort in the fact that I had been able to make a life for myself—a good life—and to finally be clear-eyed about the events that had shaped me.

A key element of this clarity came from the understanding that I could not repair the brokenness of my family or make it whole. Like Humpty Dumpty, it could never be fixed. Accepting this was the first step in putting the desire and the damage behind me. In the end, it is really not what life gives to you that matters, but what you give to life, to the people near to you. Those of us with wounds have choices. If we choose right, we have much to offer to others who are making their way through life's minefields.

The closeness I now felt to Melanie resulted from our being able to cut through the fictions of what we had been through and share the reality, for better or worse. How refreshing that was! The love we felt for each other gave me a peace I never had before. What I felt about all that had happened was beautifully expressed in one of my favorite songs by the Canadian poet, Leonard Cohen. The song was called "Anthem," and what I felt was captured in its most famous line, "There is a crack in everything; that's how the light gets in."

In an interview, Cohen explained these words. He said,

"This is not the place"—meaning this world—"where you make things perfect.... There is a crack in everything that you can put together.... But that's where the light gets in, and that's where the resurrection is and that's where the return, that's where the repentance is. It is with the confrontation with the brokenness of things."

That was exactly what I felt. With Melanie's love and courage, I was finally able to confront the brokenness of my family and let in the light that made it possible for me to finally see myself as I was.

One morning after all this happened, my husband and I were in our car listening to a psychologist talking about abuse on the radio. She was advising people not to get on the emotional roller coaster of a dysfunctional individual they might have in their lives and therefore, not to enter their world of dysfunction. I thought of how many times I had gotten onto the family roller coaster to protect, deny, look for the good, ignore the bad, and hope for the love I always thought was there deep down in everyone. I thought of what I had learned—through all my suffering and pain—that the hardest thing of all is to realize that we are not the same. Not everybody is going to feel compassion as you do, or be able to love as you understand love. Encountering someone's bad side and thinking that you can just love them through it by being understanding and overlooking what they have done is also dysfunction and denial. Denial is the silence that enveloped our family's darkest secrets and permitted the crimes to happen.

The radio psychologist was saying that 90 percent of the children in detention centers had suffered traumas in childhood similar to my siblings and me. But I didn't wind up on drugs or in jail or with a life I hated, as others had. Instead, I was like the mother who called in to the show about her child, desperate to protect her. The choice is ours to make, if it is in us to make the choice.

Thinking about the past after hearing Melanie's tale, I felt like someone who had emerged from a fog of confusion into a crystal sunlight. The question Henry had tormented me with had been turned on its head. Instead of "Who am I?" the question I now asked was, "Who are *you*?" I needed to figure out who these people in my life were, before I took another step, and why they had treated me the way they had. Only after I had answers could I know how I felt about them and, more importantly, myself.

What I had learned through a world of pain might seem obvious to others, but our family web of secrecy had caused the lessons to come late to me. If those who are close to you carry hate in their hearts for you, resenting the good that comes to you, it is because they have hate in their hearts for themselves. This self-loathing can only be endured by projecting its cynical and dark judgments onto others, joining your misery to theirs. They see the successes in your life as indictments of themselves. They seek comfort in dragging you down. Consequently, the only cure for their malice may be to cut them out of your life, like a gangrenous limb. Not everyone is capable of self-reflection or change. To accept this is one of the hardest of life's lessons, but a necessary one.

My siblings are still riding the roller coaster of family dysfunction; they have grown up to be versions of Henry and Gigi—or the bad side of Gigi: self-centered, disregardful of others, steeped in a denial that protects them from confronting themselves and taking responsibility for who they are and what they have done. I don't fool myself into thinking I am perfect. I still bear the scars of my upbringing and am familiar with my flaws. But I am not without self-understanding, and I am willing to meet my critics halfway or more. I am secure in knowing that I have compassion for others and a respect for the facts.

I have not seen my sisters and brothers—Janie, Leslie, Tommy, Rick, or Katie—in several years and probably never will again. The loss of family is the deepest pain I have experienced in my life and has been the hardest outcome for me to accept. But I finally had come to recognize that breaking free from my dysfunctional family was the price I would have to pay for my own health and peace of mind. As long as I remained a prisoner of my family's denials and lies, I was also a target of its jealousies and hates. The choice I faced was stark and clear: I could either get back on the family roller coaster or remain on the ground and hold fast to what I have learned.

I will never again collude in versions of reality whose purpose is to turn me into a victim. If my siblings were to say the same wounding things to me today that they have throughout my life, they could not hurt me as they did before. Because I finally know I am not the problem. I know who I am and it has made me free.

As for my mother, I realize that I will never be able to resolve the contradictory elements in my relationship to her, or in her relationship to herself. I have to accept that there was a good, comforting mom, and a mom who withdrew love brutally; the good mom who made my sixth birthday such a special moment and the cold-hearted woman who left me for a bar night with her friend—the same woman who rejected me at the end of our life together because she couldn't bear to look at herself. I will never be able to understand how the two mothers were the same person, never able to resolve my feelings towards both. I will never be totally at peace with the dilemmas I face, and never able to unravel the tangled web of a family history that began long before I was born.

With the passing years, I had learned more and more about Gigi's life and had come to appreciate what a hard upbringing she had too. She was never able to recover from her primal losses—the end of her innocence, the murder of her horse, Rosie, and the death of her first-born son. Cruelties were done to her that no child should have to endure and she had wounds so deep they could never heal. Raped by her own father, she never had the professional help to deal with its consequences. Probably, her hyper-sexuality was a result of those wounds. She was drawn to abusive, treacherous men, with whom she had more children than she could handle. She was the creature of a destiny she did not make. She tried to drown her sorrows and bury her defeats in alcohol and drugs but only ended up breaking herself. She betrayed her beautiful child, Melanie, to the family predator, and who knows what other of her children besides. She was the enforcer of secrets intended to protect herself, but in the end, they protected no one and eventually drove us apart.

Yet she had given me happy memories too—like the time she made an ambrosia salad with me for a family picnic; or when I was pregnant and about to give birth and she gave me massages and maternal counsel. She was a support to me and my child when I had to work to put food on our table. She was often capable of a clear-eyed view of others, and helped to guide me through some crucial choices. Because of all these generous and caring aspects of her concern, she has an indelible place in my heart. I love her for all the good she did for me and for the injustices she suffered. I forgive her for the injuries she inflicted on me, which ultimately flowed from her pain and miss her every day. She will always be my mother, and I can never stop loving her.

I am now well into middle age and a grandmother myself. In September 2016, my son Michael and his wife, Mary, gave birth to a baby girl, Penny, and the following year, to my granddaughter, Ellie. They are beautiful little girls and I adore them and cherish every moment we spend together. In 2018, Joel and I moved from California to Colorado to be near them, a reunion with my family that has filled my days with sunshine.

At the same time, the traumas of my childhood are receding, as is the break with my birth family. The memories can still be intense at times and the pain raw. When I had to recall these incidents to write this book, I sometimes could not go on for more than a page without being wracked with the torments of the past, especially my mother's breakdowns. Recounting them, bringing into the foreground the searing details of what I experienced, I sometimes felt as though I was physically breaking apart.

Talking to others about the past, which is what this book does, bringing these long-hidden episodes to light has had a therapeutic result. The mere fact that I can talk about them has muted their effects, diminishing the hurt inside me that was bottled up all those years. I am genuinely happy now and looking back on the span of my life, I can honestly say it has been a good one. This is especially true of the quarter of a century I have spent with my husband, Joel. We have shared many pleasures together, lived through exciting times, met interesting people, and enjoyed the company of wonderful friends. My life with horses has been especially rewarding, providing me a sense of achievement that I long thought would be denied. I have been privileged to have had such an opportunity and know that, in part, it is a legacy from my troubled family.

It was the love and security provided by my marriage that ultimately changed the course of my life. Yet this blessing was not like a manna falling from heaven. The blessings of my marriage were made possible by my own decisions, even as a teenager, not to follow the family path, not to be promiscuous and reckless, but to be selective and sober and, as a young mother, to protect my son and then to seek a man who would love and protect him as well.

My rewards from these choices have been rich and bountiful, but they are also reflected in such a simple pleasure as being able to sleep through the night without bolting awake, shaking with the fear of unknown threats. All through my childhood, I was beset by these night terrors in a house where both parents were often absent. Even when our parents were home, we never knew what violence might erupt or what its consequences might be. These nightmares followed me into adulthood. Looking back now, I realize my fears were not that different from my mother's terror of aliens in the walls and under the floors.

The most important change in my life has come from the family I created. As a result of our move to Colorado, I have had ample opportunities to observe my son Michael at home with his children. My son is not at all like the brothers and sisters I have left behind. He doesn't have the rage and anger that consumes them, causing them to strike out at others, especially those to whom they are closest. I was touched by his love for his daughters, Penny and Ellie, who were three and one when I wrote my story. I was moved by the way he would sit on the floor, playing games with Penny, the older one. My heart was warmed by the encouragement he gave her. "You can do it, Penny," he would say in the middle of a game. These were words I never heard in the household I grew up in. I could see how my son put his children's needs in front of his own, a basic instinct even of animals, but absent in my family upbringing. And I saw the trust my grand-daughter put in him, secure in his care.

Watching my son spend time with his daughters and shower them with paternal love, I could not help but reflect on how different this household was from the one I grew up in. Observing the care with which my son treated his children, I thought to myself: *The cycle of craziness is broken*. When my grandchildren are old enough to read this book, the world described, which I inhabited as a child, will be utterly strange to them. This is my reward for all I have been through. My son and his daughters are freed from a family legacy that was handed down through generations to mine. The trail of our suffering has come to an end.